Innovation and Entrepreneurship in State and Local Government

Edited by
Michael Harris and Rhonda Kinney

LEXINGTON BOOKS
Lanham • Boulder • New York • Toronto • Oxford

LEXINGTON BOOKS

Published in the United States of America
by Lexington Books
An imprint of The Rowman & Littlefield Publishing Group, Inc.
4501 Forbes Boulevard, Suite 200, Lanham, Maryland 20706

PO Box 317; Oxford; OX2 9RU, UK

British Library Cataloguing in Publication Information Available

The hardback edition was previously catalogued by the Library of Congress as follows:

Innovation and entrepreneurship in state and local governments / edited
by Michael Harris and Rhonda Kinney.
    p. cm.
  Includes bibliographical references and index.
  1. State governments—United States. 2. Municipal government—United
States. 3. Local government—United States. I. Harris, Michael, 1956–
II. Kinney, Rhonda, 1967–
    JK2443.I56 2003
    352.3'67—dc21

                                                        2003011716

ISBN 0-7391-0705-4 (cloth : alk. paper)
ISBN 0-7391-0926-X (pbk. : alk. paper)

Printed in the United States of America

⊖™ The paper used in this publication meets the minimum requirements of American
National Standard for Information Sciences—Permanence of Paper for Printed Library
Materials, ANSI/NISO Z39.48–1992.

Innovation and Entrepreneurship
in State and Local Government

STUDIES IN PUBLIC POLICY

Series Editor: Paul J. Rich, Policy Studies Organization

Lexington Books and the Policy Studies Organization's **Studies in Public Policy** series brings together the very best in new and original scholarship, spanning the range of global policy questions. Its multi-disciplinary texts combine penetrating analysis of policy formulation at the macro level with innovative and practical solutions for policy implementation. The books provide the political and social scientist with the latest academic research and the policy maker with effective tools to tackle the most pressing issues faced by government today. Not least, the books are invaluable resources for teaching public policy. For ideas about curriculum use, visit www.ipsonet.org.

Public Policies for Distressed Communities Revisited, edited by F. Stevens Redburn and Terry F. Buss

Analyzing National and International Policy: Theory, Method, and Case Studies, by Laure Paquette

Developmental Policy and the State: The European Union, East Asia, and the Caribbean, by Nikolaos Karagiannis

Policymaking and Democracy: A Multinational Anthology
Policymaking and Prosperity: A Multinational Anthology
Policymaking and Peace: A Multinational Anthology
Three-volume set edited by Stuart Nagel

Equity in the Workplace: Gendering Workplace Policy Analysis, edited by Heidi Gottfried and Laura Reese

Politics, Institutions, and Fiscal Policy: Deficits and Surpluses in Federated States, edited by Louis M. Imbeau and François Pétry

Innovation and Entrepreneurship in State and Local Government, edited by Michael Harris and Rhonda Kinney

Dedication

We would like to dedicate this book to our families—to Tali Harris, Ronen, Asaf, and Amit, and to Paul Longworth, Donald and Linda Kinney, Lee and Linda McWilliams, and Thomas Kinney—who bring true meaning to our lives. Their constant love and support have made this book possible. We are truly grateful.

Contents

Foreword:
Putting Entrepreneurship on the Policy Agenda

Entrepreneurship in the public sector is a viable alternative to privatization, as this carefully researched book effectively demonstrates. The interest in promoting innovation and entrepreneurship in state and local government has gained strength in recent years, through the initiatives of the Kauffman Foundation Center for Entrepreneurial Leadership, efforts at the University of Maryland and at the University of Southern California, work by the National Consortium of Entrepreneurship Centers, and programs sponsored by the Nasdaq Stock Market, to name just a few of the players in the fast growing field of entrepreneurial scholarship.

That interest in this topic has surged relatively recently shows that prejudice indeed precedes progress. A sort of folkloric misunderstanding about what government does or can do has hampered governments from displaying entrepreneurship. Coached to act in staid and bureaucratic fashion, civil servants frequently have proven the law of self-fulfilling expectations. This volume provides ample case material for the study of how we can, to use a now popular phrase, let the state back in. Of course, the state has never left and it is unlikely that even the most extreme libertarianism will send government institutions into retirement in any dramatic way—no matter how much talk there is of privatization as a panacea. The estimate of what privatization can do has been far too optimistic. State and local governments can do things well in the future that they haven't yet thought about doing at all. The best, if simple, example of this possibility that I can cite from personal experience looks to European town halls, which offer excellent restaurants and art that the general public patronizes. It is perhaps a minor example, but I have often wondered why city fathers in the United States were grimly determined, with few exceptions, to make their surroundings as dreary as possible. Few tourists put the local government headquarters in American cities high on their list of attractions—but consider visiting Stockholm and not stopping by its magnificent town hall. We still have a lot to learn from others.

Which is why this study will help a great many people who do want to revitalize government at the state and local level. Privatization is not the entire answer to providing services, and this is a bright collection full of useful ideas that will be basic to any consideration of the subject for years to come. It is a volume that could easily comprise the core reading for a course on the subject. Universities certainly need such courses. We are extremely grateful to Professors Michael Harris and Rhonda Kinney and their contributors. The Policy Studies Organization is especially pleased to have this title in its growing series of important policy books.

Paul Rich
Editor, Lexington Books' Studies in Public Policy series
President, Policy Studies Organization

March 2004

Acknowledgments

Several individuals helped us during our research and writings; we wish to thank them all, but in particular those with whom we have collaborated over the years in research upon which we rely in this book. They include Mark Daniels, Ytzhak Katz, Gideon Doron, Linda Beail, Cary Covington, Bernard O'Connor and TeResa Green. Our thanks go to three representatives from our publisher, Lexington Books: Serena Leigh, for her belief in the value of the book, and Megan Bradley and Hedi Hong, whose editorial expertise was of profound assistance. Sharon Crutchfield is deeply appreciated for her valuable support and help with editing, coordination, and communication. Sara Vangieson assisted with research and provided administrative support and Susan Campbell coordinated scheduling. Jason Mitchell and Steven Jackson provided us with assistance in locating source material. Several friends were instrumental in providing a supportive environment: Barry Fish, Bernard O'Connor, Joe Rankin, Stuart Karabenick, Ken Rusiniak, Laurence Smith, Susan Moeller, Pat Doyle, Marty Shichtman, Sally McCracken, Bette Warren, Julie Booten, Marcy Canby, Russell Larson, Laura George, and Kenneth Kidd. We would also like to thank Eastern Michigan University for its support.

Chapter 1

Michael Harris
Rhonda Kinney

Introduction

One of the biggest mistakes you can make in life is to
accept the known and resist the unknown.
You should, in fact, do exactly the opposite.
Challenge the known and embrace the unknown.
Guy Kawasaki, Cofounder Apple Computer, Inc., 1996

This book examines innovation and entrepreneurship in government. Three general issues motivate our interest in a renewed study of these matters, their interactions, and their role in public policy making. First, we observed with interest the manner in which innovative approaches to Medicaid service delivery in our home state of Michigan progressed easily throughout the recession of the early 1990s but then slowed significantly as conditions of economic prosperity persisted throughout the last half of the decade. Unlike the tight budget conditions of the 1980s and early 1990s, the late 1990s witnessed budget surpluses, low inflation rates, and economic expansion. We looked to the research literature for help in understanding this ebb and flow implementation process but did not find clear guidance. Instead, we found the literature on innovation, entrepreneurship, and risk taking in the public sector to be limited. Previous research studies seemed to look at economics and innovation in conflicting and somewhat restricted, narrowly defined ways. We hope to expand these definitions here and more fully examine innovation and policy making as they relate to economic conditions. We suggest that during times of relative economic scarcity, the demand for, and ability of, governments to introduce and effectively implement innovations increases. On the other hand, during times of economic prosperity, the risk found in introducing innovations increases as any significant change brings with it the potential to affect prosperity in a negative way. Politicians are therefore more concerned about introducing innovative policy alternatives. Why rock the boat when the economy is going well? We explore these questions through a series of case studies examining innovation at both the state and local levels.

Our second motivation relates to the tremendous expansion of interest in the areas of innovation, change, and entrepreneurship throughout the private sector. Books and articles on these topics abound in the scholarly literature on business and in trade publications. Many of these works begin with assumptions that significant change is inevitable, leaders must envision change, and to be successful they must proactively seek and manage change. These studies necessarily focus on the impact business leaders have had on change and innovation over time and the potential for such influence in the future. While one of the defining characteristics of American government has been its penchant for the status quo, modern government could not help but be affected by this pervasive attention to innovation and change among a group of its more prominent and active constituents. Given the increasingly blurred line between private and public sector management, we wondered what insights this growing literature might provide us when examining governmental innovation. We hope to begin this process of examination here.

In particular, this book reflects our recognition that policy making and innovation must take into account not only economic conditions but also encompass the role of individual entrepreneurial abilities and commitment. The challenge in incorporating these factors lies in theorizing the incentives for public sector actors to behave in entrepreneurial ways. In the business sector, entrepreneurship is grounded in the desire to maximize profits. This relationship does not easily apply in the public sector. Understanding innovation in the public sector is therefore a much more complex endeavor. Why undertake experimentation and risk in this environment? With this analysis, we hope to more fully understand the potential motivators and barriers to innovation in the public sector. We wonder why public sector officials innovate at all given the potential for failure? How concerned are government officials and politicians in taking risks? Is the risk propensity of these officials influenced by the economic outlook of their governmental unit? We also acknowledge and hope to explore more fully the influence of institutional structure and design on individual decision making and the policy-making process more generally. While we do not answer all of these questions here, we do attempt to further the dialogue regarding the role of such activities in producing innovative public policy change.

A third important influence on our choice to analyze innovation can be found in the concept's potential impact on the public's faith in governmental ability to successfully deal with problems of the day. Since the 1960s, levels of public trust and confidence in government have been in decline. For the most part, the public is skeptical of government's ability to address significant economic and social challenges. Even those who support government intervention and involvement believe that government is at times ineffective and unnecessarily costly in its approach to problem solving. Further compounding this concern is the fact that the history of business in the United States is marked by technological innovation and by entrepreneurs who took advantage of those opportunities. Americans have faith in progress and innovation as effective means by which to deal with problems and concerns. They also tend to believe in the ability of individuals to impact institutional success and achievement. Individuals such as George Eastman, Andrew Carnegie, Henry Ford, and Bill Gates have had a profound impact on economic development and prosperity. We are led to ask if we, as students of public policy, have done enough to better understand how these factors operate in the public sector. What might a better understanding of private sector thoughts regarding innovation and entrepreneurship offer us in theorizing about innovative policy making? Would trust and confidence increase if governments were more likely to innovate and were successful in implementing innovative policy solutions? Again, we do not endeavor to answer all of these questions here. However, we do hope to spur attention to the multitude of issues surrounding innovations, entrepreneurship, and public policy making.

Governments do innovate. The case studies summarized here will demonstrate that government agencies and departments can, in fact, be creative in addressing problems. Public policy analyses, both applied and theoretical, would benefit significantly from a better understanding of these innovations and from increased familiarity with the factors that correlate with innovative behavior throughout the stages of the policy-making process. Among academic researchers there appears to be a striking lack of consensus regarding the specifics of the origin, development, and implementation of policy innovation. Some important factors and frameworks have been neglected and need more attention. We hope to clarify these differences and fill in gaps in our theoretical understanding of the subject. A limited disciplinary approach will not enable us to fully grasp the dimensions of innovation in public policy making. Our approach therefore necessarily draws on literature in areas beyond public policy studies and we proceed using a complex set of interactive variables.

Governments and Change

Much of the research literature on policy making by American government emphasizes stability, incremental change, and bias toward the status quo—rightly so. We recognize the American governmental system's structural bias in favor of the status quo. Change is difficult—especially fundamental and lasting change—and requires the marshaling of tremendous will and resources. As a result, throughout its history, governments at all levels in the United States have observed long periods of policy stability broken up only occasionally by periods of great policy activity and innovation. However, in the midst of this relatively resistant environment, change does occur. In this volume we focus attention on just these exceptions. Our interest lies with explaining policy innovations and their correlates. We attempt to explain deviations from the static periods of policy innovation in the context of state and local governments. We study questions such as: "When does innovation occur?" and "What factors spur innovation and what factors hinder it?" and "What role do entrepreneurs and leaders play in fostering these change processes?"

Our study focuses on innovation within the context of state and local government policy-making. As we noted above, the decade of the 1990s witnessed policy changes particularly at the local and state government levels. These changes both drew attention from policymakers and have acted as a catalyst for research and study of innovative policy change among scholars in many fields of study. Interestingly, older policy studies typically viewed states and localities as somewhat backward and particularly slow to change. Hayes offers a representative view:

> All in all, our state and local governments are superbly equipped to do tomorrow what they did yesterday. But these governments are not designed to be highly efficient, responsive, flexible, or innovative. Any effort in this direction must run against the momentum of the system. This government structure has little surplus energy to devote to change and innovation . . . new programs and ideas move slowly and fitfully in a climate that is essentially hostile and alien to them. (1973:8)

Roscoe Martin argued that state leaders display an "addiction to the status quo" which, "leads almost invariably to an unfavorable reaction to anything new or strange" (1965:79). Scholars looked to a number of explanations for this lack of responsiveness including inadequate budgets and other resources, ineffective incentives and evaluation systems for officials, their rural and small town backgrounds, and a lack of public attention to, or support for, innovative approaches (Feller and Menzel 1978).

However, owing to the dearth of empirical data employed, these studies may have underestimated state and local innovative activities (Feller and Menzel 1978). Sharkansky maintains that states have been creative and effective (1978). For his seminal work on the diffusion of innovation, Walker found a substantial number of innovative cases for study across the nation and noted that the pace of innovation was increasing over time (1969). Certainly, a cursory examination of sub-national policy making during the decade of the 1990s suggests that the view of resistant state and local governments is not fully accurate. In fact, Republican policy makers suggested throughout the 1980s and 1990s that states and localities were brewing with new ideas and once released from federally imposed constraints would innovate even more extensively. At present, the federal government is recognizing those innovators and entrepreneurs in policy change. So, we argue that the sub-national government environment is relevant (at a minimum) and perhaps central to an understanding of innovative policy making and the diffusion of these policies over time.

The literature of policy innovation has identified a number of explanations for decisions to innovate but we note that some especially interesting avenues have not been pursued in the depth we think desirable. For example: We see economic conditions as variables in the decision to innovate and in the development and success of innovation. Further, we note that the role played in innovation by individual entrepreneurs has not been explored to the degree we need for a complete understanding of the process.

Another important dimension often missing from studies of innovation is the importance of institutional rules and structures that affect the development of policy solutions. We attempt to bring factors such as intergovernmental institutions, relationships, and decision making into the exploration of innovation in the policy-making process. Recent experience showed us that innovation could occur throughout the phases of the policy-making process including creation, development, implementation, and termination and we should be mindful of this fact as we conceptualize innovation. Innovation is not a single decision point or action (innovate or not)—it is a process. Innovations are demanded, specified and developed, implemented, evaluated, and at times, terminated. Processes can be innovative as can be the termination of one approach in favor of another.

We devote the remainder of the introductory chapter to several tasks. First, we **offer a definition of innovation** that draws together a number of conceptualizations currently found in the research literature. Second, we **review and elaborate on relevant questions and topics drawn from the research literature** on policy innovation, public policy process in general, and private sector innovation. We conclude the chapter with a **preview of the volume's subsequent chapters** and central themes.

Defining Innovation
Given the array of definitions found in the research literature for what constitutes policy innovation, it is important at this early stage to define what we mean when we use the term "innovation." We hope to employ a definition that is sufficiently clear but adequately inclusive of important facets of the term. We believe that to be innovative a policy change must fulfill the following criteria:
1. **Originality and Newness.** The policy change must be original and new to the environment in which it is being presented.
2. **Practical Application and Action.** Innovative ideas must be acted upon and applied to real-world situations and problems. We are not discussing ideas that are not implemented at all.

3. **Significance and Impact.** Innovative change moves beyond incremental change. To be truly innovative, policy change must be significant and measurably different from the status quo operating system.

Clearly, as the current research on innovation indicates, any definition of "innovation" must include originality as a key component. Rogers defined innovation as "any idea that was perceived to be new by the individual considering adoption of the idea." In evaluating "newness" the focus lies within the environment of the person considering the policy itself. Implicit in Rogers' approach is an additional and valuable distinction between invention or discovery of an idea and innovation, which requires the perception of newness by the adopter (1983). Walker (1969) and Gray (1973) applied this conceptualization specifically in the area of public policy making, including as innovative any "law, which is new to the state adopting it" (1174; see also Nice 1994).

Mohr's work on innovation in organizations expands on this, defining innovation as: *"the successful introduction into an applied situation of means or ends that are new to that situation* (emphasis in original, 1969, 112)." In developing this definition, Mohr dealt explicitly with the distinction between invention and innovation. He noted that while "[i]nvention implies bringing something new into being; innovation implies bringing something new into use" (1969, 112). Altshuler and Zegans offer a straightforward definition that builds on the distinction between invention and innovation. They view innovation as "novelty in action." Their definition incorporates the dimension of implementation, suggesting that innovation consists necessarily of both original ideas and practical action to implement these ideas (1997, 73).

Moore, Sparrow, and Spelman employed a definition highlighting the notion of importance, suggesting that innovation is "any *reasonably significant* change in the way an organization operates, is administered, or defines its basic mission" (emphasis added, 1997, 275). They, like Mohr, also make a point to include both means and ends as possible areas where innovation may occur. In operational terms, the distinction between an innovation and a marginal adjustment in ongoing operations is not always clear. No precise criteria exist to direct these determinations, but March and Simon provide some initial guidance, "Innovation [is] present when change requires the devising and evaluation of new performance programs that have not previously been part of the organization's repertory" (1958, 174-175). So, to look at a hypothetical example: In the area of Medicaid, an incremental increase in a state's Medicaid program budget, or staff numbers, would not qualify as an innovation. However, a move to introduce managed care for all covered individuals would be innovative even if the overall budget and staff number remained level from year to year.

Our study of innovation applies a definition that is broad enough in scope to include each of the ideas mentioned above. We classify as innovations any policies, programs or processes new to the entity adopting them, no matter how old the program may be or how many other units have adopted them. So for our purposes here, policy innovation refers to the process of adoption and implementation of new programs or methods of governing. Innovation may be achieved through the introduction of new or different laws, regulations, or bureaucratic practices and procedures. In defining what is "new," we focus on the context in which the policy is to be implemented. In our view, the fundamental characteristic of any innovation is the difference it creates from current policy or from standard operating practices and existing routines. We do not require that a policy change be perceived as successful for its inclusion as an innovation. In fact, one of the following chapters addresses the subject of evaluating success of innovations. We argue instead that innovation must be considered across the stages of the policy process and may succeed or fail to differing degrees across these stages. One may successfully pass an innovative program only to fail in later implementation processes.

Our definition of innovation includes changes and processes that expand the size and scope of government. We explicitly include those efforts intended to reduce the scope of government, leave size unchanged and that change the manner of implementation. We believe these innovations to be as worthy of analysis as innovations that expand government activity.

Our analysis attempts to draw some preliminary conclusions about the particular relationship between economic conditions and the form that innovation takes at the state and local level. The acceptance of a correlation between the two allows us to assume that there may be many variables indicative of an environment conducive to policy innovation. A number of explanatory frameworks exist in the research literature on policy making that may shed light on the question of what measurable variables exist when conditions are conducive to innovation? Or conversely, what factors exist that might make innovation less likely? We begin by taking a look at studies that focus specifically on policy innovation and progress and then continue on to studies of broader policy making process. We synthesize the two areas of study by arguing that innovation is not altogether separate from the traditional policy-making process and that theories of innovation should necessarily be consistent with those of the policy-making process. Some cases of regular policy-making can be specified as innovation and vice versa. Therefore, the development of our approach here draws on both sets of research.

Innovation Research
While the innovation literature appears to have moved towards a general consensus in defining the concept of innovation, the same cannot yet be said regarding approaches to explaining innovation. Studies examine various facets of innovation in differing governmental contexts. Not surprisingly, the conclusions reached have not always been consistent.

Much of the research literature on policy innovation falls into one of two distinctive approaches to explaining variation in the adoption of innovative changes in policy at the state and local level. The first general approach focuses on factors endogenous to the jurisdiction in question. These studies suggest that the primary factors leading some units to innovate are characteristics of the units themselves. Variables of interest include political, economic, and societal conditions in the states and localities.

The second group of studies focuses on the geographic diffusion of innovative policies and the degree to which different units are more or less "innovative" than others. Diffusion models regard policy innovation as a process characterized by emulation and following the leader. Some units inspire others to adopt policy changes over time. Grupp and Richards (1975) refer to this process as decision making by analogy. There has been some disagreement across studies about the scope of the scanning process individual units use in reviewing their environment but they agree that innovation is an interactive one where units compare and learn from each other over time.

Endogenous Explanations
As we suggested above, the first general approach to explaining choices to implement innovative policy changes looks to characteristics within the unit. An implicit assumption of these endogenous determinants models is

that policy-making processes across states or localities are fully independent. *This suggests that no governmental unit significantly influences any other.* These explanations generally have been tested with cross-sectional regression (or probit) models where the dependent variable is either some measure of how early a state adopts a policy among the population of potential adopters, or whether or not the state has adopted the policy by a certain date. Independent variables are internal political, economic, and social characteristics of states. Political variables of interest have included political party control of the executive and/or legislative branches of government, the impact of divided control, and political ideology.

Economic hypotheses include the idea that governments possessing slack resources would innovate more frequently than those who do not. Others suggested however, that economic scarcity and crisis motivated change. Social variables have included measures of state culture, poverty, and education levels. Considerable support has been found for various internal determinants explanation and they merit further examination here (Walker 1969; Regens 1980; Canon and Baum 1981; Glick 1981; Filer, Moak, and Uze 1988).

As we mentioned above, a number of specific variables have been examined to explain the choice to innovate. Initially, some sense must emerge that a "problem" exists for action to occur (Cyert and March 1963; Eyestone 1977; Nice 1994). The problem may be perceived or real, big or small, but its presence is often necessary for a government to move forward in the innovation process. Political factors are also variables likely to impact decisions to innovate since innovations consistent with the prevailing beliefs and values are more likely to be adopted than those that threaten those values (Nice 1994).

Based on a review of recent literature, *The Innovation Journal* lists seven major, and for the most part endogenous, factors as contributing to a resistance to innovation and risk taking among public servants.

1. *Accountability and criticism:* Politicians demand that public servants be held accountable for departmental actions; a perception that public servants who make mistakes will pay a heavy price.
2. *Infrastructure:* Initiatives to promote empowerment as a necessary condition to innovation have been inadequate.

3. *Empowerment and rules:* Political, bureaucratic, and media reactions to initiatives seen as irresponsible decisions to ignore rules have contributed to maintaining risk aversion in the public service. As well, the continuing development of generalized controls to ensure that resources are not mismanaged are often perceived by the public servants as proof that they are not trusted to make the right decisions.

4. *Capacity issues:* When managers are asked to undertake changes, often quickly and under enormous political pressure, there is neither the time nor the resources to be innovative.

5. *Innovation as a value:* The new public service values of innovation and risk taking are often perceived as clashing with the traditional values of accountability and neutrality.

6. *Innovation as a skill:* Innovation is a skill developed through experience, education, and training. Many senior managers in government have not acquired the education and experience required to promote the capacity to innovate and to take sensible risks among their staff.

7. *Need for guidance:* It has not been made clear to public servants how traditional public service values of accountability can work together with new values of entrepreneurship and innovation. (*The Innovation Journal*, 2002)

What all of these studies suggest, then, is that internal challenges and opportunities for innovation exist in policy making environments. While other factors may also explain policy innovation, much current research points to the importance of endogenous factors in understanding these chores.

Other issues can be viewed as variables indicative of future innovation. One of the most controversial issues in the research literature is the degree to which the availability of resources affects innovation. Some argue that slack resources are one key to innovation. Available funds, underutilized personnel and equipment or similar resources need to be present in the environment for reform to occur (Walker 1969; Bingham 1976; Downs and Mohr 1980).

Other scholars, particularly those who study innovation in private sector organizations or those with a more private sector orientation, suggest that innovation is propagated by the need to survive (Leonard and Straus

1997). They take an evolutionary perspective suggesting, "[i]nnovate or fall behind: the competitive imperative for virtually all businesses today is that simple." Peters (1990) and Beck (1992) echo these views. Statements such as these raise the question of whether the impending downfall of an organization, or obsolescence of a policy, might be viewed as variables indicative of a situation ripe for innovation.

One of the most neglected aspects of endogenous determinants models is the impact of institutional structures, relationships, and rules on the policy process. Institutional approaches to studying the policy process have made a huge impact on the research literature in general but are given less attention than one might suspect in this area of study. Institutional rational choice approaches to the policy process share a focus on the ways in which institutional rules impact the behavior of rational individuals motivated by material self-interest. The general framework is broad in scope and has been applied to important policy problems in the United States (Ostrom 1986, 1990; Ostrom, Gardner, and Wynne 1993, 1994; Scholz, Twombley, and Headrick 1991; Schneider, Larason, and Ingram 1995; Chubb and Moe 1990; Dowding 1995; Scharpf 1997). What we hope to highlight here is a need to include more explicit study of the ways in which institutional rules, structures, and relationships impact decisions to motivate, the success of these decisions, and their implementation and evaluation over time.

Downs and Mohr (1980) offered a number of prescriptions for improving the stability of research findings on innovation. One of their specific suggestions was to center attention on the attributes of the innovations themselves. Innovations vary by cost. Some require large expenditures of funds for personnel, equipment, and other supplies. Other changes are comparatively inexpensive. Innovations may also vary with respect to their potential impact on operating rules and behaviors. Some changes would be relatively compatible with existing systems and orientations. Others would require drastic or troublesome changes. Innovations may also differ in their accessibility to public understanding. One may incorporate complex, esoteric technology while another may be comparatively simple to understand and execute. Innovations contrast in terms of whether they can be tried on a limited, experimental basis rather than requiring a large commitment that will be very difficult to terminate. A change and its effect may be visible and dramatic or may be noticed only by a few people (Rogers 1983; Zaltman, Duncan, and Holbek 1973).

We argue that, in terms of interactions with internal characteristics, propensities to innovate may be dependent on the nature of change. Conditions such as the number and influence of the people involved as innovators and proponents for change are considered. Members of the organization under change, or the policy-making committee affect the odds of innovation by their knowledge, acquisition of knowledge, and their exploitation of that knowledge (Cohen and Levinthal, 1990). Hamel and Prahalad express similar views in stating that absorption (of knowledge) and integration (of knowledge) are central to successful innovation (1994, 131). Also important are internal factors such as the history of change in the organization and the organizations that hold sway over the organization attempting innovative change and their support or lack of change.

The frameworks discussed thus far have all focused on explaining policy change within a given political system or set of institutional arrangements (including efforts to change those arrangements). The next set seeks to provide explanations of variation across a large number of political systems.

Policy Diffusion
Policy diffusion models tend to treat a number of innovations at once, aggregating some set of decisions to innovate (or not to innovate). All policy diffusion models share the view that governmental units are more likely to adopt a policy innovation as the number of influential actors adopting the policy increases. The models differ, however, on a number of related fronts. First, studies differ in how they specify the universe of actors policy makers scan for inspiration. Some authors propose a regional diffusion process while others view diffusion as a national phenomenon. Regional diffusion studies suggest that governments focus on nearby units when scanning their environment. National diffusion models suggest that states and localities scan nationally for innovative ideas. Second, studies differ in the degree to which they concern themselves with "innovativeness" in general or within particular policy areas.

In his groundbreaking study, Walker (1969) employed factor analysis to isolate groupings of states with similar patterns of adoptions across eighty-eight policies. He then reviewed the sets in order to determine whether or not the groupings clustered by geographic region. Walker found five rough regional alignments. He identified the groups as: (1) South, (2) New England, (3) Mountains and Northwest, (4) Mid-Atlantic and Great Lakes, and (5) Border, Great Lakes, and California—indicating that states that are near each other did tend to adopt policies in a similar area over time.

Gray offered an early test of the national diffusion model (1973). She presumed that a national communication network of policy-making officials exists. Officials interact freely and share ideas across units. This communication process inspires nonadopters to act over time. As a result, the probability that a nonadopting unit will adopt an innovation in a given year is proportional to the number of interactions its officials have with officials of already-adopted units (Gray 1973, 1176). Gray (1973) and Feller and Menzel (1978) found that the timing of adoptions of several state policies, including Aid to Families with Dependent Children programs, civil rights laws, education policies, and highway technology, conformed to the pattern predicted by these diffusion models.

Grupp and Richards further refined these findings. They analyzed survey data drawn from a national sample of state officials and found that officials clearly did identify a set of highly esteemed states. Further, elite policy makers looked to these states for inspiration in policy making. However, their work suggested that the set of aspirational peers varied significantly by policy area (1975).

Based on these aggregate data studies, we can safely conclude that:

- When looking at data aggregated across policy areas and time, some states or localities clearly do move more quickly to adopt new innovations than others do (Walker 1969; Gray 1973; Savage 1978).
- When looking at individual governmental units, speed of innovation will vary significantly across policy types (Gray 1973).
- It is unclear if a governmental unit's general or policy specific innovativeness varies over time. Longitudinal studies haven't sufficiently examined the degree of change in this area over the long term.

Recently, some attempts have been made to draw together the explanatory power of endogenous determinant and diffusion models. For example, beginning in 1990 Berry and Berry have argued that when considered individually, endogenous determinants and diffusion frameworks are each deficient. They suggest that any realistic explanation of policy innovation needs to take both approaches into consideration. They note that even

early, groundbreaking studies recognized that the "pure" models were unlikely to serve as complete explanations for innovation; both Walker
(1969) and Gray (1973; see also Canon and Baum, 1981) introduced—
and found support for—both internal determinants and diffusion centered
explanations for innovations examined. However, in each of these studies,
the empirical tests of the two models presented relied on the traditional
"single-explanation" methodologies when testing hypotheses. Consequently, for each model, the empirical test failed to offer any "control" for
the causal factors specified in the other model.

In contrast, Berry and Berry introduced a fruitful methodology, event
history analysis, which permitted more rigorous empirical testing of models that incorporated both internal determinants and diffusion measures
and explanations. They find that in the cases of state lotteries (1990) and
state taxes (1992) policy adoptions are influenced by both endogenous
determinants and regional diffusion. In fact, Berry (1994, 52) suggests
that based on simulation studies "these single-explanation methodologies
frequently produce results that are wrong. The danger does not seem to be
"false negatives;" there is no evidence that the traditional tests for the
presence of regional diffusion, national interaction, or internal determinants fail to show an impact when one exists. However, "false positives"
abound; my results show a tendency for single-explanation methodologies
to detect the presence of both internal determinants and national interaction when neither is present and when, instead, policy adoptions follow a
purely regional diffusion pattern."

Policy Entrepreneurs
Until recently, scholars have made little effort to model how individual
political actors influence innovation adoption and diffusion. A few exceptions exist. Downs and Mohr found that innovation is most likely to occur
in organizations populated by motivated, imaginative, managers with good
interpersonal skills and who were willing to take calculated risks. Harris
and Kinney found that entrepreneurs were important in fostering innovations in areas of Medicaid and immigration policy (Kinney and Harris,
2001).

Mintrom has led the way in developing a model incorporating the key
role of policy entrepreneurs in the innovation process. He suggests that
entrepreneurs serve an important role in many cases of innovation. They
are skilled political actors who work to destabilize the political environ-

ment in a way that creates opportunities for change. They reframe issues, construct arguments, maximize the opportunities to sell their ideas and influence decision makers to change policy in desired ways. Frequently, these activities require entrepreneurs to engage in significant networking in and around government with the primary purpose of providing quality information about circumstances and policy options (1997, 42-43).

At times, the controversies within the innovation literature have distracted researchers from considering how we might place these discussions within the larger public policy research literature as well as within a cross-disciplinary framework dealing with innovative decision making. The public policy literature might help better explain the factors that foster and sustain policy innovation and diffusion. Mintrom suggests two general forms of opportunities for developing such connections. First, drawing on the public policy literature might suggest ways to augment our current analyses. In particular, general policy studies point to intergovernmental relationships that would make interesting avenues for research. Second, the growing positive theory literature on agenda setting and legislative behavior might offer insights at the state and local level as well (1997, 41-42).

As we mentioned earlier, research on private sector innovation offers an additional source of thought and research neglected by previous studies of public policy innovation. This literature reinforces and expands upon many of the subjects addressed in our review so far but highlights most effectively the relative lack of attention paid to proactive leadership of change in studies of public policy innovation. In contrast to public policy studies, business analyses often begin with the assumption that innovative change is fundamental to success and build from there addressing issues of leadership, context, and motivations. We do not provide a comprehensive review of this literature here. However, we do discuss below illustrative and important studies of innovation and leadership from the business literature in order to begin the process of integrating these approaches into a fuller understanding of public policy innovation.

Preeminent management expert Peter Drucker suggests that "[m]ost innovations . . . result from a conscious, purposeful search for innovation opportunities, which are found only in a few situations" (2002, 96). He suggests several areas of potential opportunity: unexpected occurrences, incongruities, process needs, industry and market changes, demographic changes, changes in perception, and new knowledge (1985, 2002). He goes on to argue that only through systematic analysis and knowledge of these sources and their context is innovation likely to occur. "Above all, innovation is work rather than genius. It requires knowledge. It often requires ingenuity. And it requires focus. There are clearly people who are more talented innovators than others, but their talents lie in well-defined areas . . . hat innovation requires is hard, focused and purposeful work. If diligence, persistence, and commitment are lacking, talent, ingenuity, and knowledge are of no avail" (2002 102).

Sethi, Smith, and Park also emphasize the important role played by managers in promoting innovative thinking about problems. "[T]eams encouraged by management to be venturesome came up with the most innovative products. These teams were invited to deviate from routine problem solving approaches and pursue untried ideas—in contrast to teams expected to embrace continuous improvement practices that build incrementally on established product development strategies" (2002, 17). Quinn (1985), Amabile (1998), Williams and Miller (2002), and Levitt (2002) also highlight the importance of leaders in establishing organizations that channel good ideas and creative energy effectively for change. These studies all point to a need to more carefully examine leadership, particularly entrepreneurial leadership, as it relates to innovative policy making. In private sector analyses of innovative decision making, the substantive focus lies with leadership. Based on this we argue that at minimum a closer look may be in order for public sector research.

(General) Theoretical Frameworks of the Policy Process

The Stages Heuristic
Perhaps the most influential framework for understanding the policy process has been the "stages heuristic" or what Nakamura (1987) termed the "textbook approach" to thinking about the public policy-making process. The model has been further developed by Jones (1970), Anderson (1975), and Brewer and deLeon (1983), and continues to shape the ways in which we conceptualize the process in the research literature.

This approach views the policy process as a series of stages, one following another in a linear, chronological fashion. The typical progression of stages consists of: agenda setting, policy formation and legitimization, implementation, and evaluation. This approach to thinking about the policy process has served a useful purpose in that it divides the very complex policy process into discrete and manageable stages. Studies abound in the literature dealing with the individual "stages" and the factors affecting the process within each stage. Notable studies include: agenda setting (Cobb, Ross, and Ross 1976; Kingdon 1984; Nelson 1984) and policy implementation (Pressman and Wildavsky 1973; Hjern and Hull 1982; Mazmanian and Sabatier 1983).

Problems/Criticisms

A significant level of recent criticism exists regarding the stages heuristic and this approach to conceptualizing the policy-making process. The work of Sabatier (both alone and with Jenkins-Smith) provides the most comprehensive critique (1993; 1999) of the approach, suggesting that "[t]he conclusion is inescapable: The stages heuristic has outlived its usefulness and needs to be replaced with better theoretical frameworks" (1999, 7). Sabatier and Jenkins-Smith offer the following specific concerns about the stages approach:

1. The heuristic is not really a parsimonious causal theory. The model as it has been developed to date fails to specify causes or driving factors within and between identified stages. No clear mechanism is presented for what causes movement from one stage to the next. As a result, research within this tradition on each of the stages has developed independently and without reference to knowledge about other stages. Thus, the approach provides only a rule of thumb and not a clearly defined theory. It is useful in processing information, but not in explaining it.
2. Because of the lack of explanation concerning the interrelation of stages or causation, the theory doesn't apply to true cases and situations. One cannot test the "stages heuristic" on actual policy innovations to see if it actually holds together as a theory. For example, evaluations of current policies influence on future agenda setting, policy formation and legitimization is at times interwoven with implementation (Nakamura 1987; Sabatier 1999).
3. The model is too narrow in focus. Sabatier and Jenkins-Smith suggest its focus is legalistic [and] top-down, viewing innovation with respect to particularly noteworthy bills or legislation (1993). The stages approach does not provide adequate detail with respect

to bureaucratic operations that affect policy innovation (Hjern and Hull 1982; Sabatier 1986; Sabatier 1999).

4. The model inaccurately views the cycles of stages as discrete with a definite beginning and a definite end. Sabatier and Jenkins-Smith suggest that a more fitting approach might be to "focus on multiple, interacting cycles involving multiple levels of government" (1993, 6).

5. The model is over simplified in that it does not explain the effects of policy analysis or "policy-oriented learning throughout the public policy process." This limits the study of policy innovation and splits the remaining study into two smaller encampments based on either the actors or processes involved in policy innovation.

Clearly, this critique is well developed and we agree to some degree with the criticisms raised by Sabatier and Jenkins-Smith. However, we believe that remedies may exist that could resuscitate certain aspects of the approach and that could make use of studies grounded in certain stages as defined by this textbook notion of policy making. More importantly for us at this point though is the understanding that innovations, as we've defined them here, are crosscutting phenomena and can occur throughout the stages of the policy process. Much can be learned from the more general research grounded in the stages approach in thinking about explanations for what spurs or detracts from successful innovation. The chapters that follow deal with all phases of the policy process where innovations are present throughout.

One question left unanswered by the literature to date is the normative value of innovation itself. Our governmental system is posited on the value of wide consensus before change, while our private sector deeply values innovation and change. Economist William Baumol raises similar questions for today's businesses (2002). While justly celebrating the positive results of our "free market innovation machine" he also attempts to moderate the romantic view of innovation in American business. The analyses of public sector innovation presented here do not presuppose that innovation is "good" or "desirable" in the same way that the private sector studies do. We leave further analysis of this topic for other scholars.

Our Own Model of Innovation

Our model of policy change applies both endogenous and exogenous factors in an attempt to explain innovations at the state and local levels. We believe this model:

- applies to a number of varying governmental contexts (e.g., both state and local governments)
- more explicitly incorporates intergovernmental incentives
- includes a wider array of innovation types
- more explicitly specifies where and how entrepreneurs fit into the picture

Figure 1
Model of Policy Innovation Process

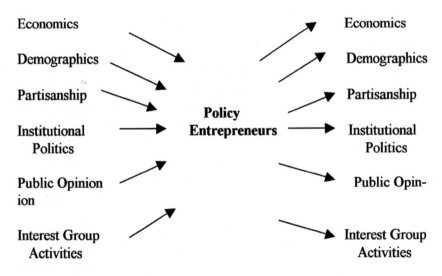

Economics   Economics

Demographics   Demographics

Partisanship   Partisanship

Institutional   **Policy**   Institutional
Politics   **Entrepreneurs**   Politics

Public Opinion   Public Opinion   ion

Interest Group   Interest Group
Activities   Activities

Demand Formation → Catalytic Conversion → Policy Specification

Policy Innovation Process

Having defined innovation as a change or reform process we need a model of innovation that reflects this process orientation. Figure 1 offers a graphical representation of how we view the innovation process. The framework attempts to bring a dynamic element explicitly into the mix as well as to clarify that some factors impact the innovation process at more than one point over time. Previous studies, while noting some of these varying effects in their discussion, do not specify them clearly in theoretical terms. Below, we also sketch in some detail the relationships summarized in figure 1 and discuss explicit relationships that are to be examined in the chapters that follow. We deal with the model's elements in time order: demand formation, catalytic conversion, and policy development.

Demand Formation

Economic Factors
Research on the effect of economic factors tends to focus on the question of what particular economic conditions spur innovation. Some analysts suggest that good economic performance correlates with policy innovation while others point to economic crises as the more common impetus for significant reform. Those who suggest that good economic times inspire innovation theorize that good economic performance leads to "slack resources" and these excess resources allow room for new, innovative policy changes. Proponents of this viewpoint cite the Great Society programs and their antecedents as examples of how good economic performance inspires policy innovation (see Nice 1994 for a review of these studies). Other analysts take the view that poor performance and economic crises lead to policy innovations. Only downturns provide the motivation required for innovations to occur (see, for example, cases in Gold 1995). We suggest that significant changes in either direction—prolonged success or longer-term poor performance—likely contribute to the formation of demand for policy change. It is during times of high citizen confidence or low citizen confidence, not during "average" times that the impetus for change emerges. We further suggest that economic conditions are quite often necessary, if not sufficient conditions, for innovation to occur.

Demographic Factors
Policy change is also likely to be driven by the demographic characteristics of the population in question—particularly shifts in these areas over time. Factors such as a state's population size, racial and ethnic mix, gender ratios, and citizens' religious beliefs are all likely to impact demand levels for policy innovation. In California, an influx of native Spanish speakers led to changes in education policy over time. States in the upper Midwest have had to face the consequences of slow population growth

and an aging citizenry in recent decades. Also, portions of the population provide varying political resources and make differing political demands of their governments. Our model incorporates these demographic influences, suggesting again that significant changes in demographic variables over time is likely to result in an increased demand for policy innovation.

Partisanship

Partisanship has been discussed in the literature primarily in terms of comparative regimes. For example, studies typically examine questions like—Do Republican regimes inspire relatively more or less innovation than Democratic regimes? (Belle 1992a; Mintrom 1997; Peterson 1990-91). There has also been some interest in the possible effect of whether or not the state was led by the same party holding the national presidency (Belle 1992b). In the area of partisanship, we again find the distinction between demand formation and policy choice stages to be helpful in thinking about relevant relationships. When it comes to demand for policy innovation, we see no particularly compelling reason to expect that there will be differential effects of Republican or Democratic leadership per se. We suggest that Democrats and Republicans are equally likely to demand policy change.

The question is really relationship to status quo. We suggest that changes in partisan regime are likely to inspire policy innovation, and this becomes more likely the longer the departing regime has been in place. Democrats coming into power after several terms of Republican leadership are likely to possess and reflect a demand for policy innovation and change. The reverse is also likely to be the case.

Other Demand Related Factors

Other variables will also likely impact the demand for policy innovation at the state level. We introduce them as control issues here but they deserve more complete attention in any full model of innovation. First, the demand for innovation at the state level will be affected by *institutional relationships* at the state level and across levels of government. For example, demand for changes in state welfare policies will be related in part to state court decisions, federal court decisions, and congressional and presidential decision making. As these institutional actors change over time, the demand for state innovations will be impacted accordingly. These issues have received scant attention in the research literature to date. Light suggests that decision makers look to actors at other levels for inspiration and guidance in the innovation process, particularly actors at the national level. In fact he suggests conceptualizing innovation as an interstate rather than simply a state-level process. He highlights the importance of the financial relationships across levels of government along with other formal means of regulatory control in shaping the innovation process (1978).

The demand for policy innovation will also be related to changes in public opinion over time. Stimson, among others, has discussed changing public policy moods, suggesting that the aggregate public experiences differentially "liberal" or "conservative" moods over time in response to current policies and conditions. As the public mood shifts, demand for innovation is likely to shift as well. Elazar (1972) is emblematic of those who have pointed to cultural and ideological factors related to state geography that will also likely impact policy innovation. Finally, interest group interest and activity will likely affect demand for innovative changes in policy (see Ringquist 1993).

Catalytic Converters and Policy Specifics

Policy Entrepreneurs

Mintrom defines policy entrepreneurs as "people who seek to initiate dynamic policy change" (1997, 738). Drawing on the agenda setting literature, he suggests that entrepreneurs promote their ideas by "identifying problems, networking in policy circles, shaping terms of policy debates and building coalitions." As the model in figure 1 illustrates, we classify entrepreneurs as catalysts in the innovation process. Collins (1999) refers to catalytic mechanisms as those that move organizations away from the status quo. As catalytic elements in the innovation process, entrepreneurs bring together, and endeavor to organize, disparate influences that build demand for policy change. Entrepreneurs attempt to systematically process and integrate these elements of demand in order to facilitate policy reform and innovation. To be successful, as in business, entrepreneurs must efficiently and effectively identify emerging problems, be prepared to take risks to promote innovative approaches, "cope with uncertainty about an innovation" (Rogers, 1983), and have the inclination and ability to organize others to help turn policy ideas into concrete programs (Mintrom 1997). While entrepreneurs are not absolutely required for innovation to occur, their activities certainly dramatically increase the likelihood innovation will occur. The entrepreneur's ability to focus demand and facilitate its conversion into specific policy proposals also streamlines the innovation process. It is important to note that not all demand will be converted into an innovative program change or even into a specific proposal for change, although entrepreneurs increase the likelihood of both tremendously.

Policy Specification

As noted above, entrepreneurs facilitate the conversion of demand into specific policy proposals. Demand for change alone will not lead automatically to innovation. Somehow demand must be focused and a specific policy innovation proposed. The set of factors that impact demand for change are also likely to affect the specification of policy alternatives. Take, for example, *economic factors*. A recession may create a demand for policy innovation. However, once that demand is focused, a potential solution must be prescribed. That solution will likely be based, at least in part, on an assessment of the underlying economic basis for the economic slowdown. Depending on the cause, the solution proposed may be cutting interest rates, balancing a budget by cutting programs, or to deficit spend in order to get the economy moving again. Here, an assessment of the current economic situation influences both demand and policy specification in distinct ways.

Partisanship will also affect the shape of innovations proposed. This is the point in the process where simple partisanship matters. By this we mean that when it comes to specifying particular solutions to identifying problems, the outcome will depend on whether the specification effort is led by Republicans or by Democrats. To use current conditions as example, Republicans will be more likely to put forward market-based innovations. Conversely, Democrats will tend towards redistributive or government-focused innovations. The details of innovation will also depend on what other institutional actors choose to do, as well as on public and interest group support levels for particular programmatic choices.

The Plan of the Book

We've presented a framework flexible enough to accommodate a wide variety of innovations. We have also developed a framework for explaining what makes some states or localities more likely to adopt innovations than others. It is now the onus of the reader to study the subsequent chapters. These chapters present case studies and examinations that provide opportunities for the reader to examine the frameworks' predictions more closely.

As will become clear, the cases do not constitute a random sample of policy areas or of states and local governments across the United States. They do, however, span much of the responsibility of state and local governments. Health care, poverty assistance, education, and economic development are all represented in the analysis, as are more general examinations of state and local policymaking. Obviously some important policy areas are not included here. However, the policy domains and geographic areas covered in the following chapters provide enough variation to offer opportunities for representative conclusions.

In chapter 2, Michael McLendon examines three case studies of policy change in higher education governance structures during the 1990s. Drawing on these studies, he offers conclusions that point to the centrality of economic conditions, particularly economic distress in motivating the innovative reform process. This chapter also highlights the importance of entrepreneurial activities in driving innovations in public policy in higher education.

In chapter 3, Richard Chard systematically examines the waiver process whereby states obtain permission from the federal government to experiment with policy delivery in ways that vary from those allowed under current federal legislation. In particular, Chard is interested in federal waivers of section 1115 of Title XIX, an amendment to the Social Security Act dealing with the Medicaid program. His chapter offers a quantitative analysis which points to the importance of intergovernmental factors, economic conditions, and the importance of states in pushing forward innovative solutions to policy problems in this area.

In chapter 4, Lawrence Grossback analyzes the use of state level mandates for local governments in Minnesota. Of particular importance here is the idea of policy reinvention—the process by which policy solutions evolve over time as states learn from previous adoptions and increased information and feedback. Grossback focuses on the importance of intergovernmental relationships and institutions but also examines other political, economic, and social variables in this context.

In chapter 5, Robert Stoker examines the governance structures of empowerment zones in Baltimore, Maryland. There, the quasi-public Empower Baltimore Management Corporation works in conjunction with resident controlled Village Centers and local, state, and national government agencies to spur economic development in the zone areas. Stoker details both the successful efforts to put these structures into place as well as the difficulties that later resulted from the complex relationships involved. He also discusses the effects of varying economic capacities of the neighborhoods included in the zones.

In chapter 6, Marilyn Klotz examines a set of case studies of innovative policy change in the area of poverty relief. In her analysis of these six studies from a midwestern state, Klotz looks closely at the role public-private collaborations play in the policy changes in question. She notes the impact of institutional design at the local level, economic and political conditions within the states and localities she examines.

Finally, in chapter 7, Douglas Ihrke and Richard Proctor turn our attention to the influence of administrative leadership on governing board behavior in Wisconsin. They explore the factors that contribute to managerial innovation at the local level. In particular, they attempt to explain the manner in which administrative leadership and board behavior serve as intervening variables affecting the perceived success of policy innovations.

We conclude the volume with a chapter that assesses the degree to which the cases we present are consistent with predictions of our general framework of innovation and the existing literature on innovation, entrepreneurship and public policy. We also attempt to identify issues regarding policy innovation left undeveloped in our model and in need of further study. We then provide a set of tentative generalizations regarding areas of particular interest to us: the central importance of economics in motivating policy innovation, the role entrepreneurs play in converting opportunities and demand for change into concerted action, the role of institutional design and relationships, particularly the vital interplay and diffusion between levels of government that serve to motivate other levels to innovative action.

Bibliography

Agnew, John. 1980. "Overview." In *Innovation Research and Public Policy*, ed. John Agnew. Syracuse: Syracuse University Press.

Altshuler, Alan A., and Marc Zegans. 1997. "Innovation and Public Management: Notes from the State House and City Hall." In *Innovation in American Government*, eds. Alan Altshuler and Robert D. Behn. Washington D.C.: Brookings Institution Press.

Amabile, Teresa M. 1998. "How to Kill Creativity." *Harvard Business Review* (Sept.-Oct.), Product Number 3499.

Anderson, James. 1975. *Public Policy-Making*. New York: Praeger.

Baumgartner, Frank, and Bryan Jones. 1993. *Agendas and Instability in American Politics*. Chicago: University of Chicago Press.

Baumol, William J. 2002. *The Free Market Innovation Machine*. Princeton, N.J.: Princeton University Press.

Beck, N. 1992. *Shifting Gears: Thriving in the New Economy*, Toronto: Harper Collins.

Berry, Frances Stokes. 1994. "Sizing Up State Policy Innovation." *Policy Studies Journal* 22 (Autumn): 442-456.

Berry, Frances Stokes, and William Berry. 1990. "State Lottery Adoptions as Policy Innovations: An Event History Analysis." *American Political Science Review* 84 (June): 397-415.

Berry, Frances Stokes, and William Berry. 1992. "Tax Innovation in the States: Capitalizing on Political Opportunity." *American Journal of Political Science* 36 (August): 715-742.

Bingham, Richard. 1976. *The Adoption of Innovation by Local Government*. Lexington, Mass.: Lexington Press.

Bingham, Richard. 1977. "The Diffusion of Innovation among Local Governments. *Urban Affairs Quarterly* 13 (December): 223-232.

Brewer, Gary, and Peter deLeon. 1983. *The Foundations of Policy Analysis*. Monterey, Calif.: Brooks/Cole.

Canon, Bradley, and Lawrence Baum. 1981. "Patterns of Adoption of Tort Law Innovations: An Application of Diffusion Theory to Judicial Doctrines." *American Political Science Review* 75 (December): 975-987.

Chubb, John, and Terry Moe. 1990. *Politics, Markets, and America's Schools*. Washington, D.C.: Brookings Institution.

Cobb, Roger, Jennie-Keith Ross, and Marc Ross. 1976. "Agenda Building as a Comparative Political Process." *American Political Science Review* 70 (March): 126-138.

Cohen, Michael, James March, and Johan Olsen. 1972. "A Garbage Can Model of Organizational Choice." *Administrative Science Quarterly* 17 (March): 1-25.

Cohen, W. M., and D. A. Levinthal. 1990. "Absorptive Capacity: A New Perspective on Learning and Innovation." *Administrative Science Quarterly* 35, 128-152.

Collins, Jim. 1999. "Turning Goals into Results: The Power of Catalytic Mechanisms." *Harvard Business Review* (July-August), Product Number 3960.

Cyert, Richard and James March. 1963. *A Behavioral Theory of the Firm.* Englewood Cliffs, N.J.: Prentice Hall.

Dowding, Keith. 1995. "Model or Metaphor? A Critical Review of the Policy Network Approach." *Political Studies* 43 (March): 136-159.

Downs, George, and Lawrence Mohr. 1980. "Toward a Theory of Innovation." In *Innovation Research and Public Policy*, ed. John Agnew. Syracuse: Syracuse University Press.

Drucker, Peter. 1985. *Innovation and Entrepreneurship: Practice and Principles* New York: Harper and Row.

Drucker, Peter F. 2002). "The Discipline of Innovation." *Harvard Review* (August): 95-104.

Dye, Thomas. 1966. Politics, Economics, and Public Policy. Chicago: Rand McNally.

Dye, Thomas. 1991. *Politics in States and Communities*, 7th edition. Englewood Cliffs, N.J.: Prentice-Hall.

Elazar, Daniel. 1972. *American Federalism.* 2nd edition. New York: Crowell.

Eyestone, Robert. 1977. "Confusion, Diffusion, and Innovation." *American Political Science Review* 71: 441-447.

Feller, Irwin, and Donald C. Menzel. 1978. "The Adoption of Technological Innovations by Municipal Governments. *Urban Affairs Quarterly* 13 (June): 469-490.

Filer, John E., Donald L. Moak, and Barry Uze. 1988. "Why Some States Adopt Lotteries and Others Don't." *Public Finance Quarterly* 16: 259-283.

Glick, Henry. 1981. "Innovation in State Judicial Administration: Effects on Court Management and Organization." *American Politics Quarterly* 9:49-69.

Gold, Steven D. 1995. *The Fiscal Crisis of the States: Lessons for the Future.* Washington, D.C. Georgetown University Press.

Gray, Virginia. 1973. "Innovation in the States: A Diffusion Study." *American Political Science Review* 67: 1174-1185.

Grupp and Richards. 1975. "Variations in Elite Perceptions of American States as Referents for Public Policy Making." *American Political Science Review* 69: 850-858.

Hamel, G., and C. K. Prahalad (1994). *Competing for the Future*, Boston: Harvard Business School Press.

Harris, Michael, and Rhonda Kinney. 1998. "Economic Constraints and Political Entrepreneurship: Medicaid and Managed Care in Michigan." In *Medicaid Reform and the American States: The Politics of Managed Care,* ed. Mark R. Daniels. Greenwood Press.

Hayes, F. 1973. "Innovation in State and Local Governments." In *Report to Center for Innovation in the Cities and States,* ed. F. Hayes and J. Rasmussen, pp. 1-20. San Francisco: San Francisco Press.

Hjern, Benny, and Chris Hull. 1982. "Implementation Research as Empirical Constitutionalism." *European Journal of Political Research* 10: 105-115.

Hofferbert, Richard. 1974. *The Study of Public Policy.* Indianapolis, Ind.: Bobbs-Merrill.

Hofferbert, Richard, and John Urice. 1985. "Small-Scale Policy: The Federal Stimulus Versus Competing Explanations for State Funding for the Arts." *American Journal of Political Science* 29 (May): 308-329.

Innovation Journal, The. 2002. *Innovation in the Federal Government: The Risk Not Taken.* Public Policy Forum [accessed 03-11-02 last revised 02-18-02 http://www.innovation.cc/articles/Risk4.htm

Jones, Bryan, Frank Baumgartner, and James True. 1998. "Policy Punctuations: U.S. Budget Authority, 1947-1995." *Journal of Politics* 60 (February): 1-33.

Jones, Charles. 1970. *An Introduction to the Study of Public Policy.* Belmont, Calif.: Wadsworth.

Kingdon, John. 1984. *Agendas, Alternatives, and Public Policies.* Boston: Little, Brown.

Kinney, Rhonda S., Michael Harris and Steven Jackson. 2001 (April). "Economic Prosperity and Policy Innovation in State Government." Presented at the 2001 annual meetings of the Midwest Political Science Association, Chicago, Illinois.

Leonard, D., and S. Straus. 1997. "Putting your Company's Whole Brain to Work." *Harvard Business Review* (July-August): 111-121.

Levitt, Theodore. 2002. "Creativity is Not Enough." *Harvard Business Review* (August); 137-144.

Light, Alfred R. 1978. "Intergovernmental Sources of Innovation in State Administration." *American Politics Quarterly* 6 (April): 147-166.

Martin, Roscoe. 1965. *The Cities and the Federal System.* New York: Atherton.

March, James and Herbert Simon. 1958. *Organizations.* New York: Wiley.

Mazmanian, Daneil, and Paul Sabatier. 1981. "A Multivariate Model of Public Policy-Making." *American Journal of Political Science* 24 (August): 439-468.

Mazmanian, Daneil, and Paul Sabatier. 1983. *Implementation and Public Policy*. Glenview, Ill.: Scott Foresman. (Reissued in 1989 by University Press of America.)

Miller, Gary. 1992. *Managerial Dilemmas*. Cambridge, England: Cambridge University Press.

Mintrom, Michael. 1997. "Policy Entrepreneurs and the Diffusion of Innovation". *American Journal of Political Science* 4 (July): 738-770.

Mintrom, Michael, and Sandra Vergari. 1998. "Policy Networks and Innovation Diffusion: The Case of State Educational Reform." *Journal of Politics* 60 (February): 120-148.

Moe, Terry. 1984. "The New Economics of Organization." *American Journal of Political Science* 28 (November): 739-777.

Mohr, Lawrence. 1969. "Determinants of Innovation in Organizations." *American Political Science Review* 63 (March): 111-126.

Mooney, Tom R., and Mei-Hsieh Lee. 1995. "Legislating Morality in the American States: The Case of Pre-Roe Abortion Regulation Reform." *American Journal of Political Science* 39: 599-627.

Moore, Mark H., Malcom Sparrow, and William Spelman. 1997. "Innovation in Policing: From Production Lines to Job Shops." In *Innovation in American Government: Challenges, Opportunities and Dilemmas*, eds. Alan A. Altshuler and Robert D. Behn. Brookings Institute Press: Washington D.C.

Nakamura, Robert. 1987. "The Textbook Process and Implementation of Research," *Policy Studies Review* 1: 142-154.

Nelson, Barbara. 1984. *Making an Issue of Child Abuse*. Chicago: University of Chicago Press.

Nice, David. 1994. *Policy Innovation in State Government*. Ames, Iowa: Iowa State University Press.

Ostrom, Elinor. 1986. "An Agenda for the Study of Institutions." *Public Choice* 48: 3-25.

Ostrom, Elinor. 1990. *Governing the Commons*. Cambridge, England: Cambridge University Press.

Ostrom, Elinor, Larry Schroeder, and Susan Wynne. 1993. *Institutional Incentives and Sustainable Development*. Boulder: Westview Press.

Ostrom, Elinor, Roy Gardner, and James Walker. 1994. *Rules, Games, and Common-Pool Resources*. Ann Arbor: University of Michigan Press.

Peters, T. 1990. "Get Innovative or Get Dead." *California Management Review* 33, no. 1: 9-26.

Peterson, Paul E. 1990-91. "The Rise and Fall of Special Interest Politics." *Political Science Quarterly* 105: 539-556.

Pressman, Jeffrey, and Aaron Wildavsky. 1973. *Implementation*. Bekeley: University of California Press.

Quinn, James Brian. 1985. "Managing Innovation: Controlled Chaos. *Harvard Business Review* (May-June), Product Number 85312.

Quinn, James Brian, and Frederick G. Hilmer. 1994. "Strategic Outsourcing." *Sloan Management Review.* (Summer): 43-55.

Regens, James L. 1980. "State Policy Responses to the Energy Issue." *Social Science Quarterly* 61: 44-57.

Ringquist, E. J. 1993 *Environmental Protection at the State Level.* Armonk, N.Y.: M. E. Sharpe

Rogers, Everett. 1983. *Diffusion of Innovations,* 3rd edition. New York: Free Press.

Sabatier, Paul. 1986. "Top-Down and Bottom-Up Models of Policy Implementation: A Critical and Suggested Synthesis," *Journal of Public Policy* 6 (January): 21-48.

Sabatier, Paul. 1999. "The Need for Better Theories." *Theories of the Policy Process.* Boulder: Westview Press.

Sabatier, Paul, and Hank Jenkins-Smith. 1988. Symposium Issue, "Policy Change and Policy-Oriented Learning: Exploring an Advocacy Coalition Framework," *Policy Sciences* 21: 123-272.

Sabatier, Paul, and Hank Jenkins-Smith. 1993. *Policy Change and Learning: An Advocacy Coalition Approach.* Boulder: Westview Press.

Sabatier, Paul and Jenkins-Smith. 1999. *Theories of the Policy Process.* Boulder: Westview Press.

Savage, Robert. 1978. "Policy Innovativeness as a Trait of American States." *Journal of Politics* 40: 212-228.

Scharpf, Fritz. 1997. *Games Policy Actors Play.* Boulder: Westview Press.

Schlager, Edella. 1995. "Policy-Making and Collective Action: Defining Coalitions within the Advocacy Coalition Framework." *Policy Sciences* 28: 243-270.

Schneider, Anne Larason, and Helen Ingram. 1995. *Policy Design for Democracy.* Lawrence: University Press of Kansas.

Scholz, John, James Twombley, and Barbara Headrick. 1991. "Street Level Political Controls over Federal Bureaucrats. *American Political Science Review* 85 (September): 829-858.

Sethi, Rajesh, Daniel C. Smith, and C. Whan Park. 2002. "How to Kill a Team's Creativity." *Harvard Business Review* (August): 16-17.

Sharkansky, Ira. 1970. *Policy Analysis in Political Science.* Chicago: Markham.

Sharkansky, Ira. 1978. *The Maligned States,* 2nd edition. New York: McGraw Hill.

Shepsle, Kenneth. 1989. "Studying Institutions: Some Lessons from the Rational Choice Approach." *Journal of Public Policy* 12:355-376.

Stimson, James. 1991. *Public Opinion in America: Moods, Cycles, and Swings.* Boulder.Westview Press.

Tedlow, Richard S. 2001. *Giants of Enterprise.* New York: HarperBusiness

Walker, Jack. 1969. "The Diffusion of Innovations among the American States." *American Political Science Review* 63: 880-899.

Williams, Gary A., and Robert B. Miller. 2002. "Change the Way You Persuade." *Harvard Business Review* (May), Product Number 9969.

Zaltman, Gerald, Robert Duncan, and Jonny Holbek. 1973. *Innovations and Organizations.* New York: Wiley.

Chapter 2

Michael K. McLendon

The Political Economy of State Policy Innovation: Higher Education Decentralization

The last two decades have witnessed a wave of state policy innovation[1] in the higher education arena. American state governments have experimented with a variety of new higher education policies and programs including, for example, college financing programs aimed at helping families better afford the rising cost of a college education and post-secondary policies designed to ensure greater "accountability" in higher education by tying state dollars to campus or student performance (Hearn and Griswold 1994; Heller 2002; McLendon, Heller and Young 2001; Zumeta 2001). A third, significant kind of state policy innovation in the higher education arena, one that has received quite little systematic scholarship, involves *governance*[2] reform of public higher education systems. Between 1985-2000, state governments debated in excess of 100 proposals to reform the structural, functional, and authority patterns of their higher education systems (Marcus 1997; McGuinness 1997; McLendon and Tenhouse 2001). Although the nature and scope of these reform initiatives appear quite diverse, one discernible governance trend over the last twenty years has been that of *decentralization* of decision authority from state governmental agencies to more local levels of campus control. The decentralization phenomenon has important policy implications for the states because their investment in higher education is enormous—state governments appropriate in excess of $62 billion annually to higher education institutions. The phenomenon also holds significant implications for the higher education domain as decentralization is changing the management and finance of public higher education (Hines 2000; MacTaggart 1998).

The higher education decentralization phenomenon holds provocative theoretical implications, as well, for it affords researchers opportunities to examine the extent to which extant conceptualizations of state government innovation adequately explain policy innovation in a domain rarely studied by political scientists—that of higher education. However, little such systematic examination has been conducted. Several studies have analyzed the independent influence of higher education governance patterns on the policy innovation behavior of state governments (Hearn and Griswold 1994; McLendon, Heller, and Young 2001), but virtually no research has investigated those factors influencing state adoption of new higher education governance policies, such as decentralization regimes.

This chapter conceptualizes state decentralization of public higher education as a form of policy innovation and examines, through case studies of governance reform in two states, the factors precipitating the adoption of new decentralization policies.

Higher Education Decentralization as Policy Innovation

American federalism effectively assigns responsibility for public higher education, including the manner in which higher education systems and institutions are governed, to the several state governments. Prior to the Second World War, public institutions of higher education enjoyed rather substantial autonomy over their internal academic, fiscal, and administrative affairs; state governments played a relatively minor role in the higher education enterprise. However, during a roughly twenty-five year period dating from the early 1950s through the mid-1970s, state governments dramatically expanded the nature and extent of their regulatory reach over public higher education (Berdahl 1975; Hearn and Griswold 1994). The rapid expansion of state control resulted from a convergence of social and political forces both internal and external to higher education, including a historic surge in college enrollments, increasing sprawl in state systems of higher education, trenchant interinstitutional rivalry, and the growing regulatory capabilities of state governments. The institutionalized control of public campuses was achieved mainly through the creation and subsequent strengthening of *consolidated governing boards* and *statewide coordinating boards*. In consolidated governing boards, states achieved a highly centralized form of campus governance, whereby a single board was empowered to make all day-to-day management decisions for institutions within a particular system (McGuinness 1997). Through the mechanism of coordination, states superimposed upon campus governance structures a new entity whose responsibility was to make central academic and fiscal recommendations or decisions for an entire state. The proliferation of these agents of centralized control was rapid, indeed; in 1950, coordinating and governing boards existed in just seventeen of forty-eight states but, by 1974, only three of fifty states were without them (Berdahl 1971, 1975).

Whereas, in previous decades, the trend in state governance of higher education was universal and in the direction of centralized governmental control, the 1980s-1990s represented a period of diverse reform in state governance, often with "decentralization"[3] of higher education systems being the express goal of state policy makers (Marcus 1997; Berdahl 1998; MacTaggart 1998; Volkwein 1987). Since 1981, at least nineteen states have enacted legislation decentralizing authority over campus affairs closer to local levels of decision making. Although there is much variety in the nature and scope of decentralization reforms, states appear to have followed several distinct approaches to the devolution of decision authority. One approach is the enactment of management-flexibility legislation. Such legislation involves transfer of decision authority over select areas of institutional management (tuition, budgeting, personnel, and purchasing, for example) from the state level to the system or campus level, while leaving intact existing coordinating and governing structures. A second approach states have taken to devolve authority closer to the campus involves the disaggregation of university governance systems, such as when states dissolve centralized governing systems and establish local boards of trust in their place. A third approach to decentralization has involved the reconstituting of public universities as public corporations vested with greater autonomy from state government and possessing new corporate identity under law. Finally, a few states have decentralized by diminishing the authority of statewide coordinating agencies and delegating the former authority of those agencies to campus boards (McLendon, 2003).

Although an appreciable literature has arisen in description of higher education decentralization reforms in the states, little is known about the factors, conditions, or circumstances that influence a state's adoption of decentralization innovation. The accumulated research on state policy innovation, however, may serve as the basis for initial conceptualization of such likely influences.

Conceptual Framework
Political scientists have systematically studied state government innovation for at least three decades, since Jack Walker's (1969) landmark work on policy "diffusion" among the American states. Traditionally, political scientists have defined *innovation* as a policy or program that is new to the jurisdiction that is adopting it (Berry and Berry 1999; Gray 1994; Nice 1994; Walker 1969). Nice (1994), for example, defined innovation as a program new to a state, "no matter how old the program may be or how many other states already have adopted it" (p. 5). Innovation, therefore, typically is differentiated from "invention," or the process by which original policy ideas are conceived (Berry and Berry, 1999).

Two primary sets of explanations have arisen to account for policy innovation by state governments. First, "internal determinants" models assert that the principal factors leading a state to adopt a new policy or program are the social, economic, and political characteristics internal to a state. Numerous studies, drawing their inspiration from theories of organizational innovation and the idea of "slack resources" (Mohr 1969), have found that larger, wealthier, and more economically developed states tend to be more innovative. In particular, much evidence from the state policy innovation literature supports the contention that the general socioeconomic conditions of a state and its citizens influence the state's likelihood of adopting innovative policies and programs (Mooney and Lee 1995; Dawson and Robinson 1963; Dye 1990; Gray 1973; Plotnick and Winters 1985; Walker 1969). Because many government innovations cost money, the availability of large financial resources can be a prerequisite for adoption (Dye 1990). Walker (1969) extended this reasoning to suggest that states with high levels of economic development may have a greater propensity toward innovation even in areas of activity that do not require large fiscal commitments, attributing part of this tendency to the states' greater tolerance of change. Berry and Berry (1992) employed "Wagner's Law" of public bureaucracy to hypothesize that one consequence of state economic development is increased demand for government services, which in turn serves as a stimulus for policy innovation. A variety of state political features also have been found to influence policy innovation in the states. Such features include, for example, the level of governmental capacity (Hays 1996; Sigelman, Roedle, and Sigelman 1981; Walker 1969), political culture (Gray 1973; Morgan and Watson 1991; Walker 1969), interparty competition (Dawson and Robinson 1963; Haider-Markel 1998; Mintrom 1997; Walker 1969), and proximity of statewide elections (Barry 1994; Barry and Berry 1990, 1992, 1999; Mikesell 1978; Mooney and Lee 1995). As Gray (1973) noted, a fundamental assumption of internal determinants models is that states do not influence one another; i.e., innovation phenomena can be explained wholly in terms of *intrastate* influences.

By contrast, policy "diffusion" models of state policy innovation, the second major explanation found in the literature, are inherently *intergovernmental* in nature. Such models hold that states emulate the policies of their peers. Rogers (1983), in his classic work on organizational innovation, defined diffusion as the process by which an innovation is communicated through certain channels over time among the members of a social system. Political scientists have adapted Roger's definition to the study of government innovation, conceptualizing the "social system" to consist of the governments of the American states. Much research has focused on the "horizontal" migration of policies among the states; that is, policies that spread from state to state, rather than from the states to the federal government or vice versa (Berry 1994; Berry and Berry 1992, 1994; Gray 1973, 1994; Haider-Markel 1998; Hays 1996; Menzell and Feller 1977; Mintrom 1997; Mooney and Lee 1995; Walker 1969).

Two types of diffusion models exist: national interaction models and regional diffusion models. National interaction models posit that officials learn about innovative policies from their peers in other states through a national communication network (Gray 1973; Glick and Hays 1991). By contrast, regional diffusion models hold that states are influenced most by their immediate neighbors; that is, states with whom they share a contiguous border or a similar region of the nation (Berry 1994; Berry and Berry 1990, 1992; Mooney and Lee 1995; Walker 1969). Walker's (1969) work, which examined the geographic distribution of eighty-eight government policies among the states over the course of U.S. history, is a classic example of a regional diffusion approach to the study of state government innovation. Walker's analysis uncovered a "national system of emulation" (p. 898) with regional variation in policy innovation based

on imitation of bell wether states; i.e., the pattern of innovation was one
of regional leaders adopting a policy first, with other states in a given
region following suit. Of the two major approaches to studying the horizontal migration of policies, regional diffusion models predominate
(Berry 1994).

A variety of rationales are employed to explain why states might emulate one another. First, states are said to copy one another as a result of
the "satisficing" decision behavior of government officials. Given the
demands of time and incomplete information, states borrow policy ideas
from one another in an effort to simplify the complexities of public decision making (Mooney and Lee 1995; Walker 1969). Second, competitive
pressures among the states are said to provide an impetus for the interstate diffusion of policy ideas (Dye 1990; Gray 1994; Berry and Berry
1990; Peterson and Rom 1990). According to this rationale, policy emulation represents an effort on the part of states to achieve a competitive
advantage over their peers, or to avoid being disadvantaged relative to
their peers. Berry and Berry (1990), for example, contend that states
adopt lotteries in an effort to reduce the incentive for citizens to cross
state boundaries to play in another state's game, thus reducing the out-of-
state transfer of wealth. Similarly, Peterson and Rom (1990) argue that
states may decrease welfare benefits in an effort to avoid becoming a
"welfare magnet" for the poor. Berry and Berry (1990) have advanced a
third rationale for diffusion: state officials have an electoral incentive to
respond to public demand for popular programs adopted by other states
(the lottery, for example). This rationale conceptualizes "competition" in
terms of the underlying electoral pressures confronting state officials.

Recently, scholars have modeled policy innovation as a function both
of intrastate characteristics and interstate diffusion dynamics (Berry
1994; Berry and Berry 1990, 1992; Mintrom 1997; Mooney and Lee
1995). Berry (1994) has reasoned that an adequate explanation of policy
innovation must incorporate both interstate and intrastate influences, for
it is as equally unrealistic to contend that state officials are unaware of
developments occurring elsewhere in the nation as it is to think that officials are not influenced by the specific socioeconomic and political conditions of their own states. This "integrative" (Gray 1994) approach to
the study of state policy innovation is made possible by the emergence of
new longitudinal analytic techniques, which allow researchers to combine both sets of explanations into a single, unified model. Using such
integrated models, researchers have found both intrastate and interstate
influences to be significant predictors of the probability that a state will

adopt an innovative policy or program in a given year (Berry and Berry 1990, 1992; Mintrom 1997; Mooney and Lee 1995).

Although policy innovation in the American states has been the focus of systematic scholarship across a variety of policy arenas, virtually no research has examined policy innovation in the higher education arena. In particular, scholars have ignored the governance reform phenomenon in higher education, despite the recent wave of decentralization activity in the states. It is possible, however, to draw upon the extant policy innovation literature in order to conceptualize those factors that may influence state adoption of higher education decentralization policies, even if the relative nature or magnitude of the hypothesized influences are less than clear. For example, it is likely that the economic conditions of the states influence their adoption of decentralization policy, although it is unclear whether such innovation accrues to conditions of economic prosperity or scarcity. In addition to economic factors, the internal political characteristics of the states likely function as drivers of decentralization reform in higher education. Specifically, shifts in partisan control of political institutions, interparty competition, and election cycles may influence decentralization policy making for the same reasons as such factors have been found to influence innovation in other policy arenas. Lastly, it is possible that states "borrow" decentralization ideas from one another. Regional and national professional organizations[4] that disseminate policy ideas about higher education governance may serve as diffusion mechanisms of decentralization reform. Cumulatively, these various interstate and intrastate influences offer a tentative framework for use in investigating decentralization innovation.

Case Studies of Higher Education Decentralization

The remainder of the chapter reports the results of an investigation that used case study methods to examine the influences of higher education decentralization in two states: Hawaii and Illinois. Case methodology was employed as the primary research strategy of the study because the focal phenomenon—state policy innovation in higher education—is so poorly understood and involves a complex set of governmental processes for which context is a critical consideration (Miles and Huberman 1994; Yin 1994). A comparative-case strategy was employed so that cross-site comparisons derived from the multiple cases could be used to establish the range of study findings. The Hawaii and Illinois decentralization cases were selected because of their diversity. Specifically, the cases differ markedly from one another both in terms of their sociodemographic, political, and higher education-system compositions and in the nature of the decentralization measures pursued.

An eclectic mix of data, including interviews, documents, and archival records, was collected in both states. Semistructured interviews with thirty-six policy actors, collected during site visits to the states, served as an especially valuable data source. Interview informants included governors and lieutenant governors, legislators and their staff, higher education agency officials, campus presidents and administrators, and academics, the press, and other "outside" observers. Data collected from each state were transcribed, coded, and classified into patterns. The chief analytic strategy employed in the study was a form of pattern-matching (Miles and Huberman 1994; Yin 1994), whereby data gathered in each case were matched against the conceptual framework of state policy innovation articulated in the preceding section.

The case summaries that follow provide narrative accounts of recent higher education decentralization episodes in Hawaii and Illinois. Each case "begins" at a point in time prior to the enactment of the decentralization reform, and then chronologically charts the course of events surrounding the policy innovation in each state. All quotations cited are those belonging to informants interviewed for this study.

Governance Reform at the University of Hawaii

The distinguishing characteristic of public higher education in Hawaii is that it is comprised entirely within the University of Hawaii system, a statewide multicampus governing system consisting of ten campuses on four islands. However, while the system office of the University of Hawaii exercises strong authority over individual campuses, historically the system itself lacked much of the fiscal and administrative authority enjoyed by peer universities, a function of the highly centralized nature of Hawaii state government. In the spring of 1997, the University of Hawaii (U-H) held the dubious distinction of being, perhaps, the nation's most heavily regulated university. Various executive agencies exerted extensive control over key aspects of university governance, as they had since the university's founding in 1907. Numerous proposals to grant the U-H, an immensely popular institution in the state, greater autonomy had arisen throughout the twentieth century, including those debated at Hawaii's three constitutional conventions of 1950, 1968, and 1978. Academics and legislative staff also had produced, over the course of the previous several decades, numerous reports outlining specific ideas for university autonomy (Potter 1984). However, such proposals and reports merely accumulated, receiving little serious or sustained attention from elected officials.

By 1997, University of Hawaii president Kenneth Mortimer was in his fourth year in office. Mortimer was a seasoned university administrator, having served for nearly two decades in senior positions at Western Washington University (president) and at Pennsylvania State University (vice provost), where he also had been professor and director of the Center for the Study of Higher Education. As a scholar, Mortimer was well regarded for his work in the areas of campus governance, faculty bargaining, and the campus-state relationship. Mortimer had intimate knowledge of higher education in Hawaii prior to his selection as the university's eleventh president, having served as a consultant to the university. However, Mortimer's understanding of Hawaii's educational, cultural, and political landscape went beyond that of his occasional consulting. Mortimer's wife was reared in Honolulu and her father was one of the founders of the modern Democratic Party that had controlled Hawaii state government since its statehood (Daws and Cooper 1990). Throughout his first four years in office, Mortimer repeatedly had called for a "new relationship" between the University of Hawaii and the state government, but elected officials showed little interest in systemic reform of public higher education governance.

Economic Crisis and Political Urgency

By the end of the first fiscal quarter of 1997, Hawaii's elected officials and general public believed that the state's lingering economic malaise had reached crisis proportions. Hawaii had entered a seventh year of anemic growth, leading the Department of Budget, Economic Development, and Tourism to declare, in April of 1997, that the economy was in the throes of a "structural transition" (DBEDT 1997). Whereas, between 1970 and 1990, Hawaii's gross product grew at an annual rate of 3.9 percent, as compared with 3 percent growth for that of the nation, the six-year period between 1990 and 1996 saw Hawaii's gross product grow at the dismal rate of 0.5 percent annually, compared with a national growth rate of 2.3 percent. Most disturbing, however, were the economic numbers for the first quarter of 1997. The historic twin engines of Hawaii economic growth—tourism and heavy capital investment in housing and infrastructure—had begun experiencing aftershocks of the 1996 plunge of the Asian markets. Consequently, Hawaii's General Fund tax revenue for the first quarter of 1997 declined 5 percent from the previous reporting period.

Compounding the sense of crisis about Hawaii's economy were looming statewide elections, to be held in November of the following year. Although eighteen-months away, the elections already had become the focus of intense media scrutiny, both because of the economic crisis and the scope of the upcoming election cycle—one-half of the Senate, all members of the House, and Governor Benjamin Cayetano faced re-election. The political stakes were highest for Hawaii's Democrats, who held all of the important statewide offices, but who had faced increasingly stiff Republican opposition in recent years. One Democratic legislator recalled his colleagues' dismay:

> Foremost, everyone was terrified and frustrated by economic conditions at the time. We had an election coming up…it was just real bad timing. We knew the economy would be the number one issue and if something wasn't done, a few of us might not be around [in the next legislature]. That's when the *task force* arose.

Setting the Agenda for Governance Reform

In July of 1997, Governor Cayetano, the senate president, and the house speaker announced the formation of the blue-ribbon Economic Revitalization Task Force (ERTF). The ERTF was the product of backroom discussions that had taken place among Hawaii's senior Democratic leadership in the weeks following the April economic report. The task force's charge was to devise a set of proposals for invigorating the state's economy that could be incorporated into a series of bills when the legislature convened in January 1998. Named to the panel were twenty-seven individuals representing Hawaii's business and labor establishments. Included in the panel's membership was U-H president Kenneth Mortimer.

The ERTF, conducting its business behind closed doors, organized into five workgroups to develop recommendations for economic stimulus. Each workgroup was to independently develop a set of recommendations, then submit those recommendations for a vote by the larger task force when the group reconvened in plenary session. The Education and Workforce Training work group subdivided itself into two bodies, one focusing on K-12 education and a second addressing higher education. The higher education subgroup consisted of several representatives from the University of Hawaii, chairman of higher education committees in the Hawaii legislature, and several consultants on higher education issues. The focus of the higher education subgroup became singular—the development of a proposal granting the U-H more management authority. The idea originated with President Mortimer, who raised it at the subgroup's first meeting. The president's colleagues, being familiar with the frustrated history of higher education governance reform in Hawaii, interpreted Mortimer's comments about the need for greater "university flexibility" as likely to involve a devolution of decision authority from state executive agencies to the university.

The subgroup began to discuss the operational features of various alternative flexibility proposals. One idea, articulated in previous legislative studies, was that of patterning the University of Hawaii after the University of California system. This particular idea, however, was rejected in favor of transforming the U-H into a "quasi-public corporation." The idea of converting public agencies into *quasi-public* entities was a familiar one to many Hawaii legislators. Indeed, in one well publicized episode, the legislature had sought to "privatize" a state-run hospital by granting it quasi-public status, thereby empowering the hospital to manage its day-to-day affairs absent of strict state oversight. One member of the higher education subgroup recounted his colleagues familiarity with the hospital legislation, and with the recent history of privatization policy making in Hawaii, generally:

> We modeled [the university flexibility proposal] after the state hospital system being turned into an independent entity. "Quasi-public" was the [term] used at that time. The idea of turning [public agencies] into semi-private agencies had come into more common usage. Even the governor had jumped onto the privatization bandwagon. This is where the idea [for university flexibility] came from.

Recognizing that ideas about government deregulation would likely "play well" before the larger task force membership, the higher education subgroup decided to "borrow" the term *quasi-public* to refer to their as yet unspecified university flexibility initiative.

In the short period of time between the final meeting of the higher education subgroup and the reconvening of the ERTF in October 1997, the idea of reforming the campus-state regulatory relationship in Hawaii became linked with the goal of state economic development in the minds of influential business leaders who served on the task force. Informants close to the course of events attributed this critical development to the advocacy efforts of President Mortimer. Historically, efforts to achieve greater operational autonomy for the University of Hawaii were framed in terms of academic freedom; i.e., proponents of autonomy asserted that greater freedom for the university was essential to protect the core academic function of the institution. However, in the several weeks prior to the reconvening of the ERTF, Mortimer began to assert in private conservations with members of the ERTF that, if freed from excessive state oversight, the university could become more "entrepreneurial," spurring economic development in Hawaii. In his conversations with ERTF members prior to the October meeting, Mortimer employed this new rationale for university autonomy arguing that greater management freedom for the university would translate into improved economic conditions for the state. The specific freedoms Mortimer sought included the authority of the university to negotiate faculty contracts, to procure its own goods and services, to manage its budget and lands, to manage auxiliary enterprises, and to retain its own legal counsel.

When the ERTF reconvened to debate the proposed recommendations, substantial differences of opinion emerged about many of the proposals presented, especially those that called for changes to Hawaii's tax structure, consolidation of state executive departments, and privatization of public services. However, little debate surrounded the proposal to make the University of Hawaii a *quasi-public corporation*. Despite the absence of evidence or even sustained discussion within the task force about the alleged economic benefits of the university autonomy measure, the ERTF unanimously voted in favor of adding a university decentralization proposal to its package of legislative recommendations for stimulating economic recovery. Among the thirty-two proposals the ERTF announced the following day at a news conference was one to "restructure the University of Hawaii into a quasi-public corporation."

Policy Enactment

As the 1998 legislative session got under way, the issue of higher education governance reform seemed to gain irresistible momentum, aided in no small way by the controversy that began to engulf many of the other proposals put forward by the Economic Revitalization Task Force. Despite very high expectations among policy makers and the public that the ERTF's recommendations be enacted as some form of economic stimulus package, differences between business and labor interests doomed many of the proposals (Omandam 1998). Public employee unions threw the political weight of their organizations against several bills aimed at privatizing government services. Environmental and anti development activists lined up against an ERTF proposal to eliminate the Public Land Use Commission, a recommendation originally aimed at achieving cost savings through agency consolidation. Hawaii's small business owners and legislative Republicans orchestrated fierce opposition to the ERTF's most controversial proposal, a change in the state tax structure that would lower personal income tax rates, but increase the general excise tax. Barely one month into the legislative session, many of the core recommendations of the Economic Revitalization Task Force were bogged down in committee and many others were doomed to certain defeat on the chamber floors.

In sharp contrast, support for the university governance reform proposal, a relatively innocuous, inexpensive, and politically feasible idea, swelled. University officials, receiving political support from the governor and from members of the business community, developed several autonomy bills that moved quickly through legislative committee. One month into the session, higher education committees in both chambers passed similar restructuring bills; in April, conferees resolved the few remaining differences between their respective bills. In June of 1998, Governor Cayetano signed the decentralization measure, Public Act 115, into law. The governor characterized the legislation as a significant victory both for higher education and for economic development in Hawaii. Press reports called the recently enacted autonomy legislation the University of Hawaii's "Magna Charta" and designated the university "the big winner" of the 1998 session.

By all accounts, the political ramifications of Public Act 115 were significant. For embattled Governor Ben Cayetano and many members of the Hawaii legislature, passage of the governance reform legislation provided a reelection boost. The governor and senior legislative leaders of both parties characterized the governance reform initiative as one of the major victories of their political careers, and all of them made the legislation a prominent theme of their reelection campaigns. One senior university official provided the following assessment of the electoral significance of Public Act 115:

> Everyone was looking to the general election. When [the governance reform legislation] passed, it became everyone's "going-home" stuff. The governor referred to it in campaign speeches. Legislators . . . told constituents they had freed the university from excessive state regulation. Most every [incumbent] was able to say they had a hand in this bill—this bill that was the most significant development in higher education in the last half-century, this bill that would help jump-start the economy—and they didn't let voters forget it.

Five months later, Cayetano survived a close reelection challenge, as did virtually the entire Democratic legislative leadership, which retained control of both chambers of the assembly.

Decentralizing System Governance in Illinois
By 1991, Illinois's so-called "system-of-systems" approach to the state-wide organization of higher education had served for three decades as an effective device for the balancing of competing interests among sectors and institutions of higher education in that state. The system-of-systems was a complex segmental structure consisting of (1) four multicampus governing boards for public universities, (2) a community college system, (3) a private college sector, and (4) a statewide coordinating board. The four multicampus governing boards included those of the flagship University of Illinois system (responsible for two campuses), the Southern Illinois system (two campuses), the Board of Governors (five campuses), and the Board of Regents (three campuses). Although various bills calling for the elimination of the Board of Governors and Board of Regents had been periodically introduced into the legislature over the past several decades, no such bills were given serious attention by lawmakers; despite occasional resentment of a few campuses toward their respective "intermediary" boards, most legislators and campus officials were generally supportive of Illinois's well-regarded higher education system.

Challenges Confronting Illinois's "Education Governor"
In early 1991, newly elected governor James (Jim) Edgar's prospective education agenda, which he had pledged to make the top priority of his administration, was imperiled by three interrelated obstacles. First, Illinois's economy was showing signs of being seriously affected by the economic downturn that was spreading throughout the nation; state unemployment figures were inching higher as automotive sales throughout the Midwest declined. Moreover, newspapers were reporting regularly on the "recession" that would soon visit the state. A second major obstacle confronting Edgar in his effort to become Illinois's "education governor" was his pledge to hold the line on new taxes and to reduce the size of state government. Tax abatement and government downsizing had been prominent themes of candidate Edgar's gubernatorial campaign. Coupled with the economic downturn, these commitments made the prospect of increased funding for education improbable. The third challenge confronting Edgar's prospective education agenda was that Democrats had

already "cornered the market" on several prominent education reform issues, such as Chicago school reform and school finance reform, effectively denying the new administration an education reform issue of its own. One aide to the governor commented on the frustration felt by members of the governor's staff as they struggled to define the administration's education agenda:

> There was a sense both that the [education] agenda was wide open, because nothing big had been proposed in the education area in a few years, but also that the agenda was limited, because Democrats had already staked the high road on lots of hot-button education issues. So, we talked about charter schools and about school choice, but there was real concern about generating new ideas.

Cumulatively, Jim Edgar faced the daunting challenge of delivering on a campaign pledge to make education the top priority of his administration while simultaneously slashing the state budget and avoiding the embrace of education issues traditionally associated with Democrats.

The governor's three fold dilemma became manifest in his first budget proposal, which Edgar presented to the General Assembly two months after taking office. The budget provided only $30 million in new money for the state's $2.1 billion school aid allocation and no increase for higher education, a move the administration acknowledged would translate into large tuition increases at Illinois campuses. The governor's budget proposal drew immediate and sharp criticism from assembly Democrats.

Lt. Governor Kustra's "Gaffe"
In October 1991, nine months into Edgar's term and several months into economic recession, Lieutenant Governor Robert Kustra appeared before the Macomb, Illinois, Chamber of Commerce as part of a whistle-stop tour that was intended to remind citizens of the new administration's commitment to issues considered important to the business community. Instead, Kustra's speech in Macomb, home to Western Illinois University, a Board of Governors institution, helped catapult the issue of university decentralization onto the governmental agenda. One senior administration aide who attended the speech recalled:

> As a habit, [Kustra] didn't use notes when he [spoke]. So, [he] started delivering this stepwinder of a speech, without knowing exactly [what he'd] say. But, [Kustra] knew Macomb is a university town and that they wanted their local university

> to have its own board of trustees because no one liked being part of the Board of
> Governors. So, [Kustra] began talking . . . and before you know it, [he proposed]
> doing away with the Board . . . "Let's give Western Illinois the board it de-
> serves'"[he said]. But the press was there—taking notes.

The headline in the next day's local paper read, "Lt. Gov. Proposes
Shake-Up for WIU Board."

The lieutenant governor's remarks were sure to attract attention. The
administration's designated point man on education issues, Kustra was a
seasoned higher education insider. He had served as a professor of political science at several Illinois colleges. Indeed, throughout Kustra's
steady ascent in Illinois politics, he continued to hold adjunct faculty positions, including ones at Northwestern University and DePaul University. Kustra also had served for ten years as a member of the General Assembly, during which time he chaired the Senate Education Committee.
Kustra's perspective on Illinois higher education was shaped by several
episodes during the 1980s of alleged spending excesses by the Board of
Regents and Board of Governors university systems, episodes which attracted heavy press coverage about the boards' expenditure activities.
Although these various experiences had negatively influenced Kustra's
perceptions of the regional governing boards, Kustra and his aides nev-
ertheless were concerned about the political ramifications of the lieutenant governor's remarks about the boards. Upon returning to the capitol,
Kustra sought Governor Edgar's counsel. A senior administration source
present during the conversation recounted the exchange:

> [Kustra] popped [his] head into [Governor Edgar's] office and said,
> "Hey, I need to talk a few minutes here. You know how strongly I feel
> about these governance [issues]. Well, I kind of went out on a limb and
> said we should get rid of the Board of Governors and [Board of] Trus-
> tees. I was really talking off the top of my head. I don't want to embar-
> rass you." Edgar replied, "Embarrass me? I think it's a good idea. When
> will we do it?"

Governor Edgar's ready acceptance of the gaffe owed in large part to his
own past experiences with the Board of Governors and Board of Regents. Such experiences, including one in which the Board of Governors
dismissed from the presidency of one of its campuses a personal friend of
Edgar's, had soured Governor Edgar on the multicampus boards and
their leadership.

The Governor's Task Force on Higher Education

The 1992 Illinois General Assembly convened amidst intense partisan wrangling between Governor Edgar and assembly Democrats over Illinois's deeply troubled economy. Against the backdrop of a budget stalemate, the governor delivered his State-of-the-State speech on January 27, some three months after Kustra's comments in Macomb. In the speech, Edgar urged the legislature to make across-the-board budget cuts. He also floated for the first time the idea of abolishing the Board of Governors and Board of Trustees. There was little public reaction to the idea, for the state's budget woes dominated the attention of policy makers. In April, Governor Edgar presented his proposed FY1993 budget to the General Assembly, his second consecutive budget without a funding increase for universities. In the speech, Edgar returned to the idea of abolishing the Board of Governors and Board of Regents and called for the creation of a task force to study how the state could save money by "trimming the higher education bureaucracy." The following week, he announced the formation of the Governor's Task Force on Higher Education (GTFHE) and appointed Kustra as cochair. The creation of GTFHE attracted instant press coverage, with both the *Chicago Tribune* and *Chicago Sun-Times* running editorials in support of efforts to "streamline" higher education. Most observers assumed that, since the governor had already advocated abolishing the boards, the panel would quickly move toward adoption of a specific board-elimination proposal.

The task force held its first meeting in Springfield, Illinois, in May 1992 without notifying the public as to its convening. According to participants involved in the deliberations, most members of the blue-ribbon panel already were prepared to eliminate the regional governing boards; several specific proposals to that effect were discussed at the meeting. The panel agreed to reconvene in June so that a final recommendation could be forwarded to the governor. At the second meeting, which was open to the public, leaders of Illinois's four university systems testified unanimously in favor of retaining the Board of Regents and Board of Governors systems. The testimony did little to change the minds of task force members; on June 19, the panel released its report recommending that the two governing boards be abolished and that local boards of trust be established for seven of the eight campuses in the two systems. The task force report offered numerous rationales in defense of its recommendation, asserting that decentralization would reduce "bureaucracy" in public higher education, achieve significant "cost savings" through the elimination of the boards, and remedy the perceived "weaknesses" that plagued the boards, although the report did not specify the precise amount of the cost savings or the nature of the alleged weaknesses.

While little in the way of clear or compelling "evidence" existed that governance decentralization would have the beneficial effects its proponents claimed, the very idea of "decentralization" seemed to have virtue of its own. Government reform and downsizing had been effective themes of Edgar's gubernatorial campaign. Moreover, ideas about "reinventing" government were emerging as popular ones on the national political landscape (Cook 1998; Osborne and Gaebler 1992). A close observer of the Illinois episode, a legislative ally of the Edgar administration, made the following remark about the "fit" between the nature of the decentralization policy advocated by the administration and the broader popular currents of the day:

> This issue was tailor made for these two Republican leaders—Edgar and Kustra. Their administration had been looking for a way to jump-start their so-called "education agenda," and this issue was the perfect fit. It was an easy issue for them to try to pick up some political points . . . efficiency, decentralization, downsizing, ending bureaucracy . . . these messages fit perfectly [with] the tenor of the times and with a Republican ideology about devolution and smaller government . . . these] were the popular buzzwords.

The report's release cemented Republican support for "decentralizing" higher education governance in Illinois. When the General Assembly convened in January 1993, the governance decentralization bill, shepherded by the lieutenant governor, moved rapidly through the Republican-held upper chamber. However, in the House the bill encountered insurmountable opposition from the Democratic majority; House Democrats objected to provisions of the bill that would weaken the collective bargaining power of certain university employee unions. Although higher education decentralization remained a heated issue throughout the 1993 legislative session, Democratic control of the House prevented the bill's enactment.

Policy Enactment

Legislative passage of the university decentralization bill was not assured until the 1995 general session. On November 4, 1994, Illinois experienced a political sea change. On the night of the Gingrich-led Republican sweep of the United States Congress, Illinois Republicans dominated statewide elections; voters returned Governor Edgar to a second term in office, padded Republican control of the Senate, and gave Republicans a solid majority in the former Democratic-controlled House. The victory was the first time in almost three decades that Republicans controlled the chief executive's office and both chambers of the General Assembly. The proposal to eliminate the Board of Governors and the Board of Regents systems, still a personal priority of Governor Edgar and Lt. Governor Kustra, achieved immediate agenda status when, on the evening of the election, Edgar and Kustra agreed by telephone to make the decentralization proposal part of the governor's so-called "fast-track legislation." Kustra once again spearheaded efforts to pass the decentralization legislation. Although the decentralization bill introduced in 1995 was exactly the same proposal as that defeated in the 1993 assembly, the trajectory of the 1995 bill was markedly different from that of its earlier counterpart—a mere three weeks into the legislative session, the university decentralization bill was signed into law by Governor Edgar.

Study Findings
The higher education decentralization episodes examined in this investigation vividly demonstrate how the intersection of conditions of economic scarcity and electoral instability can serve as a powerful catalyst for policy innovation by state governments. In both cases, economic stagnation, turned recession, created a climate of perceived political vulnerability for incumbent gubernatorial regimes. Against this backdrop, proposals to reform public higher education systems—namely, to *decentralize* them—emerged as a partial answer to electoral crisis. Two specific aspects of the intersection of economic and political conditions attending decentralization innovation deserve mention. First, the prospect of further economic decline in both states, coupled with already stagnant economies, helped "trigger" interest among policy elite for innovation in higher education governance. It is unclear whether such interest in decentralization would have existed in the absence either of the preexisting climate of economic contraction or of the anticipated future worsening of state economic conditions. Second, innovation in higher education governance became politically feasible when other policy options for stimulating the state economy (tax reform, additional budget cuts, or the consolidation of state agencies, for example) themselves proved impracticable.

The cases do not provide evidence of a differential party effect on state innovation in higher education governance—Democratic (Hawaii) and

Republican (Illinois) regimes were equally willing to experiment with decentralization policies in the higher education arena. There is, however, abundant evidence of a decentralization-*electoral* relationship. Specifically, both Hawaii and Illinois adopted decentralization reforms in their respective higher education systems when embattled gubernatorial regimes began searching for solutions to the political problem of electoral challenge. This finding seems consistent with two elements of the conceptual framework cited earlier in the study. First, it lends support to the assertion that higher levels of interparty competition positively influence the likelihood that a state will adopt new policies and programs. The reason for this appears straightforward: politicians in states with closely contested elections adopt new policies and programs in an effort to broaden or cement electoral support (Haider-Markel 1998; Mintrom 1997; Walker 1969). As Berry and Berry (1999) astutely note, the responsiveness of elected officials to the preferences of the public should be expected to vary according to the officials' level of electoral security. In the focal decentralization cases, officials' electoral *insecurity* was enormously high, thus creating incentives for policy experimentation.[5] The finding also lends support to the notion that politicians experiment with new policies at times within their election cycle that are most politically advantageous (Berry and Berry 1999; Mintrom 1997; Mooney and Lee 1995). In both Hawaii and Illinois, decentralization legislation, which incumbents deemed to have potential political value, arose in the year of, or the year preceding, a statewide election, when politicians stood to gain the most from the prospectively popular initiatives. Although scholars have amply documented the instrumental role of K-12 education on the state political landscape (Mintrom 1997; Opfer and Wong 2002), little previous consideration has been given the possibility of a connection between statewide election cycles and higher education policy adoption.

Curiously, interstate diffusion processes do not appear to have influenced decentralization innovation in the focal cases; rather, *intrastate* economic and political forces were the primary drivers of policy innovation. The Hawaii case reveals an interesting dynamic of policy "borrowing" among different domains (from the health care domain to the higher education domain) within the state, but the dynamic was wholly internal to Hawaii. The finding that policy diffusion was not an important factor in governance innovation in Hawaii and Illinois should be balanced against the totality of the research evidence in the state policy innovation literature, evidence that appears to be accumulating in favor of a "diffusion effect" (Berry 1994; Berry and Berry 1992, 1999; Gray 1994; Haider-Markel 1998; Hays 1996; Mintrom 1997; Mooney and Lee 1995). Moreover, a recent study of higher education decentralization, one relying on a larger data set of cases than that utilized in the present investigation, has documented that policy ideas to reform public higher education systems sometimes do migrate across state boundaries (McLendon 2003), although the precise nature and mechanism of migration are unclear. One valuable task for researchers, therefore, is that of further specifying the conditions and circumstances under which policy diffusion is likely to occur.

Finally, one finding of the study made conspicuous by its similarity across the decentralization cases is the existence of *policy entrepreneurs*, whose advocacy of governance innovation heavily influenced critical phases of decentralization policy making. The notion of policy entrepreneurship has become well established in the public policy making literature, particularly in research on governmental agenda-setting (Bardach 1972; Baumgartner and Jones 1993; Kingdon 1984; Polsby 1984; Price 1971; Weissert 1991). Little systematic attention, however, has been paid to the role of entrepreneurs in policy innovation, per se (Gray, 1994). Mintrom (1997) has taken an important step in this direction through his analysis of the role of entrepreneurs in advancing the school choice issue before state policy makers. Mintrom found that the actions of policy entrepreneurs raised significantly the probability of legislative consideration and approval of school choice as a policy innovation. Building on Mintrom's work, Kinney, Harris, and Jackson (2001) characterize entrepreneurs as "catalytic elements in the innovation process, [who] bring together, and endeavor to organize, disparate influences that build demand for policy change" (p. 3).

Such characterization clearly can be made of the one or two key individuals in each decentralization case who, functioning as a kind of catalytic converter for policy innovation, mobilized the emerging economic and political conditions of their respective states in such a way as to effect substantive policy change. Policy entrepreneurs—namely, a university president in Hawaii and a governor and lieutenant governor in Illinois—were especially influential in the processes of issue redefinition and interest mobilization. In both states, these advocates of policy change effectively redefined latent governance reform ideas previously of little interest to those outside the higher education community into "decentralization" proposals couched in the language of economic development, economic stimulus, and budget containment. Although economic recession created within each state a political climate that was receptive to policy experimentation, it was the determined efforts of a few key individuals to redefine governance reform as a specific solution for state economic distress that made possible the decentralization issue's emergence on the state policy agenda. Importantly, entrepreneurs also helped specify the particular policy solutions that later took the form of decentralization legislation. Entrepreneurs played no less vital a role in the "mobilization of interest" (Baumgartner and Jones 1993; Cobb and Elder 1972) that was required for the enactment of the respective higher education decentralization policies. In Hawaii, successful mobilization involved the policy entrepreneur's leveraging of his own social standing and technical expertise to build a powerful coalition of state business elite that supported decentralization innovation. In Illinois, successful mobilization of interest involved the entrepreneurs' (1) creation of a new political vehicle (a blue-ribbon task force) by which to focus elite and mass attention on the decentralization idea and (2) their commitment to sustaining political support for the proposed innovation over time.

Conclusion

This chapter reported the results of a comparative case study investigation of the factors influencing decentralization innovation in public systems of higher education. Using a conceptual framework derived from the extant policy innovation literature, the investigation focused both on the intrastate and the interstate influences of decentralization innovation in two diverse states: Hawaii and Illinois. The chief finding of the case analysis is that decentralization innovation resulted from a complex intersection of economic and political forces internal to each state; interstate diffusion dynamics did not play a role in the adoption of the new higher education governance regimes. More precisely, states experimented with higher education governance reforms when conditions of severe economic scarcity (recession) created and compounded electoral instability (challenges to incumbent regimes) such that decentralization became a partial solution to political turbulence. The intersection of intrastate economic and political forces appears to have been a necessary, but insufficient, condition for policy innovation in higher education governance. Of critical importance was the policy entrepreneurship of a single individual or two in each case, whose formal political power or social standing, domain specific knowledge, and personal commitment to governance reform effected the adoption of decentralization policy innovation.

Endnotes

[1] Following conventional practice, this chapter employs the term, *innovation*, to mean a policy or program that is new to the jurisdiction adopting it.

[2] The term *governance* refers to the ways in which states have organized their respective systems of higher education, and authority and management patterns within those systems. Various typologies of state governance of higher education have been developed (see those by Berdahl [1971] and McGuinness [1997], for example). Most such typologies conceptualize governance patterns along a continuum ranging from decentralized, in which a single institutional board makes decisions for an individual campus, to centralized, in which state-level agencies make decisions for a group of institutions or for an entire state system of higher education.

[3] "Deregulation" and "devolution" are other terms used (interchangeably) in the literature to characterize this particular kind of governance reform activity.

[4] Among such organizations, for example, are the State Higher Education Executive Officers Association, the National Center for Higher Education Management Systems, Western Interstate Commission on Higher Education, and the Education Commission of the States.

[5] Although indices of state interparty competition typically characterize Hawaii as, historically, one of the nation's most Democratic-dominant states (see, for example, Bibby and Holbrook, 1999, 1983), the decentralization episode reported in this case study occurred at a point in time in which Republicans were poised to make substantial inroads into state elective office.

Bibliography

Baumgartner, F., and B. Jones. 1993. *Agendas and Instability in American Politics.* Chicago: University of Chicago Press.

Berdahl, R. O. 1971. *Statewide Coordination of Higher Education.* Washington, D.C.: American Council on Education.

Berdahl, R. O. 1975. *Evaluating Statewide Boards.* San Francisco: Jossey-Bass.

Berdahl, R. O. (1998). "Balancing Self Interest and Accountability: St. Mary's College of Maryland." In *Seeking Excellence through Independence: Liberating Colleges and Universities from Excessive Regulation,* ed. T. J. MacTaggert: 59-83.

Berry, F. S. 1994. "Sizing Up State Policy Innovation Research." *Policy Studies Journal* 22 (3): 442-456.

Berry, F. S., and W. D. Berry. 1990. "State Lottery Adoptions as Policy Innovations: An Event History Analysis." *American Political Science Review* 84: 395-416.

Berry, F. S., and W. D. Berry. 1992. "Tax Innovation in the States: Capitalizing on Political Opportunity." *American Journal of Political Science* 344: 715-742.

Berry, Frances Stokes, and William D. Berry. 1999. "Frameworks Comparing Policies Across a Large Number of Political Systems." In *Theories of the Policy Process,* ed. Paul A. Sabatier. Westview Press: Boulder, Colorado 169-200.

Bibby, J. F., and T. M. Holbrook. 1999. "Parties and Elections." In *Politics in the American States: A Comparative Analysis.* 7th edition, eds. V. Gray, R. L. Hanson, and H. Jacob V. Gray, R. L. Hanson, and H. Jacob. Washington, D.C.: CQ Press.

Bibby, J. F., and T. M. Holbrook. 1983. "Parties and Elections." In *Politics in the American States: A Comparative Analysis.* 5th edition, eds. V. Gray, H. Jacob, and K. N. Vines. Washington, D.C.: CQ Press.

Bingham, R. D. 1977. "The Diffusion of Innovation among Local Governments." *Urban Affairs Quarterly* 13: 223-232.

Boeckelman, K. 1992. "The Influences of States on Federal Policy Adoptions." *Policy Studies Journal* 20: 365-375.

Carnegie Commission on Higher Education. (1973). *Governance of Higher Education.* New York: McGraw-Hill.

Carnegie Foundation for the Advancement of Teaching. 1982. *The Control of the Campus: A Report on the Governance of Higher Education.* Princeton, N. J.: Princeton University Press.

Cobb, Roger W., and Charles D. Elder. 1972. "Participation in American Politics: The Dynamics of Agenda-Building. Allyn and Bacon: Boston, Mass.

Cook, C. E. 1998. *Lobbying for Higher Education.* Nashville, Tenn.: Vanderbilt Press.

Daws, Gavan, and George Cooper. 1990. *Land and Power in Hawaii.* Longitude: New York.

Dawson, R. E., and J. A. Robinson. 1963. "Inter-Party Competition, Economic Variables, and Welfare Policies in the American States." *Journal of Politics* 25 (2): 265-289.

Department of Budget, Economic Development, and Tourism. 1997. *Towards a Productivity Driven Growth Strategy.* Honolulu: Author.

Dye, T. R. 1990. *American Federalism: Competition among Governments.* Lexington: Lexington Books.

Filer, J. E., D. L. Moak, and B. Uze. 1988. "Why Some States Adopt Lotteries and Others Don't." *Public Finance Quarterly* 16: 259-283.

Foster, J. 1978. "Regionalism and Innovation in the States." *Journal of Politics* 40 (1): 179-187.

Gittell, M., and N. S. Kleiman. 2000. "The Political Context of Higher Education." *The American Behavioral Scientist* 43 (7): 1058-1091.

Glick, H. R., and S. P. Hays. 1991. "Innovation and Reinvention in State Policymaking: Theory and the Evolution of Living Will Laws." *The Journal of Politics* 53 (3): 835-850.

Graham, H. D. 1989. "Structure and Governance in American Higher Education: Historical and Comparative Analysis in State Policy." *Journal of Policy History* 1 (1): 80-107.

Gray, V. 1973. "Innovation in the States: A Diffusion Study." *American Political Science Review* 7 (4): 1174-1185.

Gray, V. 1994. "Competition, Emulation, and Policy Innovation." In *New Perspectives on American Politics,* eds. L. C. Dodd and C. Jillson. Washington, D.C: CQ Press.

Haider-Markel, D. P. 1998. "The Politics of Social Regulatory Policy: State and Federal Hate Crime Policy and Implementation Effort." *Political Research Quarterly* 51 (1): 69-88.

Hays, S. P. 1996. "Influences on Re-invention during the Diffusion of Innovations." *Political Research Quarterly* 49 (3): 631-650.

Hearn, J. C., and C. P. Griswold. 1994. "State-Level Centralization and Policy Innovation in U.S. Postsecondary Education." *Educational Evaluation and Policy Analysis* 16 (2): 161-190.

Hines, E. 2000. "The Governance of Higher Education." In *Higher Education: Handbook of Theory and Research*, vol. XV, ed. J. C. Smart. New York: Agathon Press.

Huber, J. D., C. R. Shipan, and M. Pfaler. 2001. "Legislatures and Statutory Control of Bureaucracy." *American Journal of Political Science* 45 (2): 330-345.

King, G., R. Keohane, and S. Verba. 1994. *Designing Social Inquiry*. Princeton, N.J.: University Press.

Kingdon, John W. 1984. "Agendas, Alternatives and Public Policies." Little Brown and Company: Boston, Mass.

Kinney, R. S., M. Harris, and S. Jackson. 2001. "Economic Prosperity and Policy Innovation in State Government." Paper presented at the annual meeting of the Midwest Political Science Association, Chicago, Ill.

Lowry, R. C. 2001. "Governmental Structure, Trustee Selection, and Public University Prices and Spending." *American Journal of Political Science* 45 (4): 845-861.

Lutz, J. M. 1987. "Regional Leadership Patterns in the Diffusion of Public Policies." *American Politics Quarterly* 15: 387-398.

MacTaggart, T. (ed.). 1998. *Seeking Excellence through Independence: Liberating Colleges and Universities from Excessive Regulation.* San Francisco: Jossey-Bass.

Marcus, L. R. 1997. "Restructuring State Higher Education Governance Patterns." *Review of Higher Education* 20 (4): 399-418.

McGuinness, A. C. 1997. *State Post-Secondary Education Structures Handbook.* Denver: Education Commission of the States.

McLendon, M. K. 2003. "State Governance Reform of Higher Education: Patterns, Trends, and Theories of the Public Policy Process." In) *Higher Education: Handbook of Theory and Research,* ed. J. Smart. New York: Agathon Press.

McLendon, M. K. (forthcoming). "Setting the Agenda for State Decentralization of Higher Education." *The Journal of Higher Education.*

McLendon, M. K., D. Heller, and, S. Young. 2001. "State Postsecondary Policy Innovation: Politics, Competition, and Interstate Migration of Policy Ideas." Paper presented at the annual meeting of the Midwest Political Science Association, Chicago, Ill.

McLendon, M. K., and A. Tenhouse. 2001. *2001 State Higher Education Governance Survey.* Nashville, Tenn.: Peabody Center for Education Policy, Vanderbilt University.

Menzel, D., and I. Feller. 1977. "Leadership and Interaction Patterns in the Diffusion of Innovations among the American States." *Western Political Quarterly* 30: 528-536.

Mikesell, J. 1978. "Election Periods and State Tax Policy Cycles." *Public Choice* 33 (3): 99-105.

Miles, M., and A. Huberman. 1994. *Analyzing Qualitative Data,* 2nd Edition. Beverly Hills, Calif.: Sage.

Mintrom, M. 1997. "Policy "Entrepreneurs and the Diffusion of Innovation." *American Journal of Political Science* 42: 738-770.

Mohr, Lawrence B. 1969. "Determinants of Innovation in Organizations." In *American Political Science Review* 63: 111-126.

Mooney, C. Z., and M. H. Lee. 1995. "Pre-Roe Abortion Regulation Reform in the U.S. States: Diffusion, Reinvention, and Determination." *American Journal of Political Science* 39: 599-627.

Morgan, D., and S. Watson. 1991. "Political Culture, Political System Characteristics, and Public Policies among the American States." *Publius* 21: 31-48.

Nice, D. C. 1994. *Policy Innovation in State Government.* Ames, Iowa: State University Press.

Omamdam, P. 1998. "Sizzle or Fizzle: A Look at the Bills before the 19th Legislature." *Honolulu Star-Bulletin* May 14. Honolulu, Hawaii.

Opfer, Darlene, and Kenneth Wong. 2002. "The Politics of Elections and Education." In *Educational Policy Special Issues* (January, March).

Osborne, D., and T. Gaebler. 1992. *Reinventing Government.* Reading, MA: Addison-Wesley.

Peterson, P., and M. Rom. 1990. *Welfare Magnets.* Washington, D.C.: Brookings Institution.

Plotnick, R. D., and R. F. Winters. 1985. "A Politicoeconomic Theory of Income Redistribution." *American Political Science Review* 79: 458-473.

Polsby, N. 1984. *Political Innovation in America.* New Haven: Yale University Press.

Potter, R. 1984. *Autonomy and Accountability at the University of Hawaii.* Higher Education Policy Study, No. 2. Honolulu: College of Education, University of Hawaii.

Price, D. E. 1971. "Professionals and 'Entrepreneurs': Staff Orientations and Policymaking on Three Senate Subcommittees." *Journal of Politics* 33: 316-36.

Rogers, E. 1983. *Diffusion of Innovations.* New York: Free Press.

Rosenthal, A. 1998. *The Decline of Representative Democracy.* Washington, D.C.: Congressional Quarterly Press.

Sigelman, L., P., W. Roeder, and C. T. Sigelman. 1981. "Social Service Innovation in the American States: Deinstitutionalization of the Mentally Retarded." *Social Science Quarterly* 62: 503-515.

Squire, P. 1993. "Professionalization and Public Opinion of State Legislatures." *Journal of Politics* 5(2): 479-491.

Volkwein, J. F. 1987. "State Regulation and Campus Autonomy." In *Higher Education Handbook of Theory and Research,* ed. J. C. Smart. vol. 3: 120-154. New York: Agathon Press.

Walker, J. L. 1969. "The Diffusion of Innovations among the American States." *American Political Science Review* 63 (3): 880-899.

Weissert, C. (1991). "Policy Entrepreneurs,Policy Opportunists, and Legislative Effectiveness." *American Politics Quarterly,* 19 (2): 262-274.

Yin, R. K. (1994). *Case Study Research,* 2nd edition.. Thousand Oaks, Calif: Sage.

Zumeta, W. (2001). "Public Policy and Accountability in Higher Education: Lessons from the Past and Present for the New Millennium." In *The States and Public Higher Education,* ed. D. E. Heller. Baltimore, M.D.: The Johns Hopkins University Press.

Chapter 3

Richard E. Chard

The State of Health: Innovations in Health Policy

Introduction

In this chapter, I examine how a policy innovation known as the Section 1115 waiver was used by states to reduce Medicaid costs while balancing other aspects of health care favored by the public. The goals of ensuring quality, providing universal access, and containing costs are popular. However, they remind us of the ambiguous nature of some policy legislation when it is designed for the purpose of credit claiming, rather than problem solving. Thus, these abstract objectives become interesting subjects for policy study when researchers examine how actors in the health policy arena transform these goals from ambiguous ideals into practical solutions. It is then that one realizes that these objectives are mutually exclusive and rather than full attainment of each, the art is in balancing the three. Much of the work of achieving this balance is conducted at the state level and in this chapter I examine state-based solutions to balancing health care access and quality while controlling costs.

As table 1 and graph 1 show, health care costs in the United States have increased at an increasing rate. In 1965, health care expenditures consumed approximately 5 percent of the gross domestic product and by 1999 that percentage rose to 13 (United States Bureau of the Census 2001; Congressional Budget Office 1993), nearly tripling in just three and a half decades. This has implications for state and federal governments, because, at any given time, about 31 million people are enrolled in Medicaid, the joint federal and state health insurance plan for indigents (United States Bureau of the Census 2001).

Table 1: U.S. Health Care Spending as a Percentage of Gross Domestic Product

Year	Percentage of Gross Domestic Product		Year	Percentage of Gross Domestic Product
1960	5		1980	8
1961	5		1981	8
1962	5		1982	9
1963	5		1983	9
1964	5		1984	9
1965	5		1985	9
1966	5		1986	9
1967	6		1987	9
1968	6		1988	10
1969	6		1989	10
1970	7		1990	10
1971	7		1991	11
1972	7		1992	11
1973	7		1993	12
1974	7		1994	12
1975	8		1995	12
1976	8		1996	13
1977	8		1997	13
1978	8		1998	13
1979	8		1999	13

Source: United States Bureau of the Census, 2001

For example, between 1970 and 1993 the state share of Medicaid spending rose from $2.5 billion to $41.8 billion (Levit et al. 1994). As Weissert and Weissert note, "in 1992 state Medicaid expenses took up 34 percent of the state budget in New Hampshire, 28 percent in Rhode Island, 24 percent in Tennessee, 23 percent in New York and Louisiana, and 21 percent in Indiana and Missouri . . . by fiscal year 1993 the mean state spending for Medicaid exceeded state spending for higher education . . . by $2 billion (1996: 208). For this reason, states have become laboratories for experiments in controlling costs for Medicaid in particular and health care in general.

Graph 1: U.S. Health Care Expenditures as a Percentage of
Gross Domestic Product 1960 to 1999

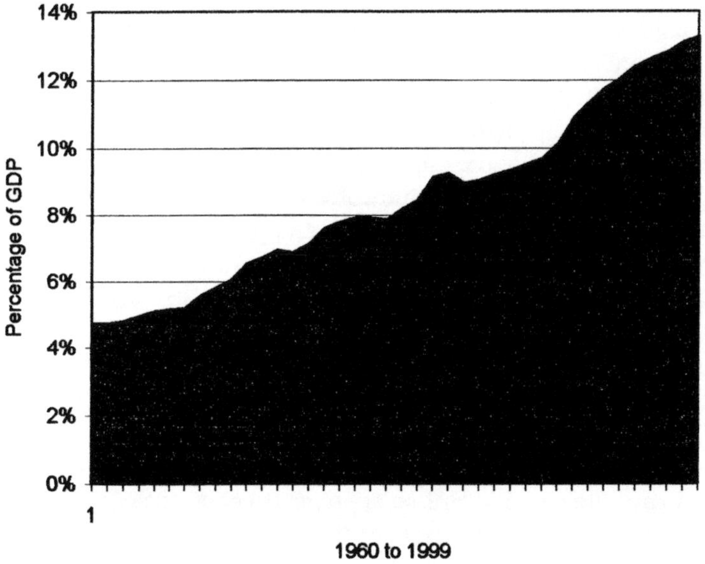

1960 to 1999

Figure 1

The basic problem of ever increasing costs rests in the simple equation that generates costs:

(Price) x (Quantity) = Costs

As with all equations containing variables, the value of these components can be changed or fixed. Such manipulations will, in theory, alter the output of the function. Attempts to limit the variables in this equation, price and quantity, could be achieved through various regulatory mechanisms. For example, price controls could be imposed, thus freezing that variable at some level. The problem with this is that the enterprising hospital or physician could simply increase the quantity of services performed, thus keeping the output (costs) level. In the same sense, attempts to limit quantity (rationing) could be circumvented by raising prices. Thus any regulatory attempt to control costs must place limits on both the price of medical services and the quantity.

The recognition that costs can be controlled only through the use of rationing and global budgeting is crucial to the success of state-sponsored health care plans. Rationing is of course restricting the usage of medical services, while global budgeting refers to allocating a specific dollar amount to health care, which is in essence rationing through budget. Specifically, in the global budgeting system, once the money is used, health care services are restricted until the next budget cycle. These are often used together in state-sponsored health care plans. For example, the British National Health Service has a budget frozen at 6 percent of the gross domestic product of the United Kingdom (Aaron and Schwartz 1984). The means of achieving this control is through price control—essentially fixing the costs—in the form of global budgeting and restrictions on the quantity supplied through rationing.

In the United States, the federal government has adopted two programs designed to control health care costs. The first was the Diagnostic Related Group (DRG) a fee schedule designed to control hospital expenditures. The other was the Resource Based Relative Value Scale (RBRVS), which was an attempt to control physician costs within the fee for service system used in both Medicare and Medicaid.

In the United States, two pioneering states, Arizona and Oregon, attempted variations on the British approach to control their own spending. In these states there was recognition that operating government-funded health insurance plans on a fee for service basis created many of the cost control problems that are present in private fee for service arrangements. Primarily cost shifting by the hospitals and physicians induced demand.

Cost shifting occurs when individuals without private health insurance who are ineligible for traditional Medicaid benefits seek care. The bills go unpaid and are absorbed by the hospital or physician who then passes it along to insured individuals through higher rates. The second is a long held assumption among health economists (see Feldstein 1993, for example) that physicians who are paid on a quantity-based scale push quantity up by ordering more tests or procedures. In managed care arrangements, physician induced demand is controlled, while universal coverage solves the problem of cost shifting.

A History of the Medicaid Program
In 1965, Congress passed Title XIX as a major amendment to the Social Security Act. This amendment established Medicaid as a medical assistance program for certain low-income individuals and families. The congressional intent in passing this legislation was to have the federal and state governments work together to finance medical assistance for the poor (Stevens and Stevens 1974). Congress believed that such a partnership between the federal government and state governments would improve the accessibility and quality of medical care among the poor and disadvantaged.

The federal government played a major role in the early development of the Medicaid program, assuming two crucial responsibilities. First, by providing matching funds to the states for the program, with the intent to encourage the states to voluntarily establish and maintain their Medicaid programs. Second, by enacting general program guidelines to ensure coordination among the programs across the states. These provisions were designed to create a framework within which each state could initiate and maintain a unified system of health care for the poor (Stevens and Stevens 1974). Within this framework states could fashion their Medicaid programs to meet their specific needs and situations. To that end, states were allowed to determine specific program-eligibility criteria, benefit packages, and service provisions, as well as provider participation policies and reimbursement levels.

Ultimately, however, the federal government took the lead in establishing the basic direction of Medicaid program growth in several key ways. First, the federal government set the regulations that determined who would be covered by the program. Initially, Medicaid eligibility was closely tied to the receipt of public assistance. In order to receive Medicaid, individuals or families had to first meet the financial requirements of the Aid to Families with Dependent Children (AFDC) or the Supplemental Security Income (SSI) programs. By keeping Medicaid closely tied to welfare, the federal government was able to preserve one of the basic ideas behind the development of the program. Medicaid, at its inception, was presented as a limited health-insurance program providing benefits to certain groups of deserving, low-income individuals and families. By setting the guidelines for eligibility, the federal government was able to ensure this limited coverage.

The federal government also determined the range of medical services that would be available to Medicaid recipients in the states. Once qualified for the program, individuals and families were supposed to receive a single package of health care benefits regardless of where they resided. The federally required services included physician care, hospitalization coverage, laboratory and x-ray benefits, and outpatient hospital care. States were allowed to prescribe additional optional services to their Medicaid populations, but the federal list of allowable optional services was restrictive and focused primarily on acute care rather than prevention. In addition, there was little flexibility for the states to pursue other, nonfederally approved forms of medical care, such as preventive services. Such restrictions made the states unwilling to expand the scope of their Medicaid services (Davidson 1980).

Similar restrictions on provider participation, service reimbursement, and utilization control affected the states' decision making in other Medicaid program areas. Federal policies specified the type of medical providers that could receive Medicaid reimbursement along with when and how they would be compensated for the care they gave to program participants. Federal regulations monitored how physicians actually delivered services to their Medicaid patients. The result of these regulations and policies was that the federal government retained a substantial amount of control over the Medicaid program.

Program Expenditure Increases—From the 70s to the 80s
Although the basic governmental structure of the Medicaid program remained intact throughout the 1970s, by the close of the decade there were significant program developments in Medicaid. Most notably, Medicaid expenditures were following the national trend for health care expenditures with rapid increases. For example, during the initial year of the program's implementation, the total cost of Medicaid came to $3 billion, by 1975, Medicaid expenditures totaled $12.2 billion, and by the start of the 1980s, total Medicaid expenditures increased to more than $29 billion, a nearly tenfold increase in Medicaid expenditures from the 1970s to the 1980s.

In addition, by the end of the 1970s, the states had begun a striking departure from each other in the ways that they implemented their Medicaid programs. Some states elected to use the discretionary authority given to them to expand their program coverage to other needy families and individuals that did not represent the federally mandated groups. Other states changed their Medicaid benefit packages by adding services beyond those federally prescribed, or by varying the ways in which the services were administered. These decisions by the states affected the size and scope of each Medicaid program, and had noticeable effects on program costs. As a result, there were dramatic differences in program expenditures from state to state, despite the fact that the original federal/state structure of the Medicaid program remained.

In the early 1980s, a shift occurred in Medicaid decision making. Policy responsibilities were transferred from the federal government to the states through the passage of the Omnibus Budget Reconciliation Act of 1981 (OBRA 81). Congress passed OBRA 81 in response to President Reagan's desire to decrease federal control over a wide range of public policies. Although, OBRA 81 did not reduce federal influence over Medicaid as much as President Reagan would have liked, it did give states an increased decision-making role over many policies.

OBRA 81 increased the scope and type of Medicaid choices available to the states. It eliminated a substantial number of federal restrictions and established new procedures that allowed states to experiment with alternative health care service delivery programs and programs for reimbursement. OBRA 81 also allowed the states to choose to target subgroups of their Medicaid populations in order to provide them with a full range of benefits.

OBRA 81 began the shift for responsibility of Medicaid oversight from the federal government to the states. Congress justified these changes by citing concerns over the "quality of care" and "health care access," and it was widely held that OBRA 81 provisions would indeed create a more effective program that would reduce spending.

By 1986 there was a plethora of changes in the Medicaid program that made it significantly easier for the states to expand their Medicaid programs to a more diverse group of needy families and individuals. The Defect Reduction Act of 1984 (DEFRA) required states to cover pregnant women and children even if they were not receiving actual cash assistance and to provide services to infants born to Medicaid-eligible women up to one year of age. The following year, the Consolidated Omnibus Budget Reconciliation Act of 1985 (COBRA) allowed the states to increase benefits and provide increased levels of care for certain subgroups of the population including pregnant women and infants. Several months after passage of COBRA, Congress enacted the Omnibus Budget Reconciliation Act of 1986 (OBRA 86), which officially ended the federally mandated link between Medicaid and AFDC. OBRA 86 allowed the states to expand their Medicaid programs to thousands of low-income women and children without increasing their AFDC coverage. This break signaled a change in the ways that health and welfare issues were viewed. As a result of this change, OBRA 86 is often viewed as the single most influential piece of legislation affecting Medicaid eligibility and coverage.

Medicaid was further revised in the late 1980s and early 1990s. Many of the changes were either expansions or modifications of earlier changes. Legislation passed in 1987 and 1990 extended Medicaid coverage to pregnant women and children up to 1.85 times the federal poverty rate and to the disabled and aged populations. States were allowed to phase in Medicaid coverage for children up to age nineteen living in families below the federal poverty level. States were also given the authority to provide home and community-based services for disabled elderly individuals and mentally challenged individuals.

Section 1115 Waivers: Experimenting with State Innovations
Outside of official federal legislative changes, one of the most active areas in state Medicaid program innovation is in the use of Section 1115 research and demonstration waivers. Ironically, the authorization for this type of state health-care policy experimentation predates the enactment of Medicaid. Three years prior to the establishment of Medicaid, Congress granted the states the ability to test innovative projects and to seek waivers of certain federal requirements that dictated the amount, scope, and duration of services provided across a state. Authorized under Section 1115 of the Social Security act, this provision covers all programs that fall within the original and subsequent jurisdiction of that act. As a result, it was immediately applicable to Medicaid once that program was authorized in 1965 as Title XIX of the Social Security Act.

Under Section 1115, states are allowed to petition for two types of Medicaid waivers: (1) research; and, (2) demonstration program waivers. Together, these two types of waivers—research and demonstration—enable the states to deviate from many standard Medicaid regulations in order to test new ideas. They are allowed to be both broad and flexible in scope, and are granted under the Section 1115 authority. The research waiver exempts states from certain general federal requirements, and are generally used to develop home and community-based programs; however, they do not give states the same degree of flexibility as do the Section 1115 demonstration waivers.

Over the past thirty years, states have used the Section 1115 demonstration waiver option to introduce a variety of innovations in their health-care delivery programs. During the 1970s, several states, including Georgia, South Carolina, New York, and Connecticut, were granted Section 1115 waivers to test ways of providing home and community-based care to elderly populations instead of nursing home care. Several states used Section 1115 waivers during the 1970s to improve access to care for hard-to-reach populations, particularly children. Other initiatives focused on managed care, although they were limited in scope and were initiated as test programs. The most well known of these Section 1115 managed care programs was developed by Arizona, which established the first statewide system of managed care for all Medicaid recipients in 1982.

These recent applications of Section 1115 waivers receive most of the attention. The original Arizona demonstration, the Arizona Health Care Cost Containment System (AHCCCS) and the copycats changed Medicaid completely from 1982 to 1996. Beginning in 1993, when the Clinton administration signaled a willingness to allow more cost-saving experiments like AHCCCS, the states proposed a record number of Section 1115 waivers and submitted more requests after 1993 than the total of all requests submitted in the preceding thirty years. These requests have been designed as ways to save money through the use of health maintenance organizations (HMOs) as with AHCCCS or extend Medicaid coverage to previously uninsured groups and expand the package of medical benefits available to program participants as Oregon did.

The Arizona Health Care Cost Containment System
and Oregon's Plan

The state of Arizona applied for a demonstration waiver (§1115) from the Health Care Financing Administration (HCFA) in the early 1980s in order to establish the Arizona Health Care Cost Containment System (AHCCCS). The demonstration waiver was granted to the state allowing it to test an alternative payment and delivery system for Medicaid enrollees. AHCCCS was implemented in 1982 and incorporated several innovations designed to achieve the overall goal of cost containment. Primarily managed care techniques such as preadmission certification and utilization review are used to keep AHCCCS costs low. Additionally, the AHCCCS plans, like health maintenance organizations in the private sector, purchase blocks of hospital care at capitated rates and then pay additional charges at discounted rates. These innovations in controlling price and quantity of health care utilization combine to effectively control costs in Arizona.

In comparison to the Arizona plan, the Oregon plan was designed to bring more people into the Medicaid system, thereby reducing uncompensated care, without increasing the cost of the plan. For this reason, Oregon applied for a demonstration waiver to develop a system that would ration expensive highly technical care such as lung transplants and funnel that money toward more primary care for more people. The Oregon plan sought to guarantee health care to all citizens of Oregon by evaluating the effectiveness of treatments. Thus the Oregon plan allowed a high quantity of low-priced procedures and restricted the quantity of high-priced procedures. This had the effect of stabilizing the cost in spite of opening Medicaid to groups not traditionally covered under that plan. While the waiver application was filed under the Bush administration, it was not until President Clinton took office that it was finally granted.

Policy Innovations and Diffusion in the States
Walker's (1969) study of why some states act as pioneers in policy innovations and how such innovations spread was one of the earliest to examine policy diffusion among the states. Walker defines an innovation "as a program or policy which is new to the states adopting it, no matter how old the program may be or how many other states have adopted it (1969, 881). Walker goes on to explain that some innovations are adopted through simple imitation of the leading state, while others are adaptations of innovations from one state designed to suit the needs of the adopting state.

Gray (1973) extends Walker's notion by defining innovation "as an idea perceived as new by an individual; the perception takes place after invention of the idea and prior to the decision to adopt or reject the new idea" (1174). Gray's primary contribution is in noting that the cumulative density of those adopting innovations follows a sigmoid curve distribution. From this, one can assert that adoptions of policy innovations among the states follow a normal distribution when plotted over time. Thus, at the beginning, there are a few pioneers who propose policy innovations—in this case Arizona and Oregon. During the middle of the series, one observes a seemingly ever increasing number of adopters followed by a trailing off until, at the end of the series, adoption stops.

Others built on these two groundbreaking articles addressing innovations across a wide range of policy areas (Grupp and Richards 1975). Scholars have focused on specific policy areas such as juvenile corrections (Downs 1976), technology (Menzel and Feller 1977) and human services (Sigelman, Roeder, and Sigelman 1981). Berry and Berry (1990) note that the research intended to answer Walker's initial question of what causes a state to adopt a new program has diverged into two schools of thought, those who favor internal factors as the explanation and those who favor regional diffusion as an explanation. The authors argue that the two are in fact compatible and demonstrate this with their construction and results of their model for the diffusion of state lotteries. Berry and Berry (1992) support this finding in another policy realm, state adoption of tax policy innovations. Generally, the authors find support for the influence of both internal and regional factors.

Taken together, the research on the diffusion of policy innovation supports the basic premise discussed above that some internal factor such as a desire to control costs leads a state to propose a change in Medicaid. This then leads other states with a similar need to mimic the first state. In 1992, only Arizona and Oregon had applied for waivers to use managed care arrangements to provide health care for Medicaid enrollees. In 1993 Kentucky and Tennessee were added to that list. By 1994, Delaware, Minnesota, Illinois, Missouri, Ohio, Florida, South Carolina, Rhode Island, Massachusetts, and New Hampshire all applied for waivers. Of these states, all were spending 21 percent or more of their state budgets on Medicaid (Weissert and Weissert 1996). In 1996 twenty-three states had been granted or had waiver applications pending before the Health Care Financing Administration for Medicaid Managed Care demonstration projects.

Empirically Analyzing the Innovation Diffusion
In order to fully understand what impacts the decision to switch to a managed care system for Medicaid, one must first theorize what factors would logically influence such action. Aside from the usual suspects such as controls for partisanship of the legislature, education, per capita income, the percentage of uninsured in the population, the number of physicians, and the prevailing daily medical charge, one familiar with the innovation diffusion literature would hypothesize an effect from a neighboring state adopting a Medicaid managed care approach. Additionally one would assume that the number of Medicaid enrollees in a given state and the cost of Medicaid benefits per enrollee would influence a state's decision to adopt a managed care approach. Thus, I propose the following model:

$$\text{ADOPT} = b_0 + b_1 \text{ NEIGHBORS} + b_2 \text{ MEDICAID ENROLLEES} +$$
$$b_3 \text{ MEDICAID EXPENSE} + b_4 \text{ UNINSURED} + b_5$$
$$\text{PHYSICIAN} +$$
$$b_6 \text{ PER DIEM} + b_7 \text{ PID HOUSE} + b_8 \text{ PID SENATE} +$$
$$b_9 \text{ EDUCATION} + b_{10} \text{ INCOME} + e$$

Variables:

NEIGHBORS: Coded as one if a neighboring state has applied for a waiver and zero otherwise.

MEDICAID ENROLLEES: The number of nonelderly people enrolled in Medicaid in a given state in thousands.

MEDICAID EXPENSES: The state expense for each nonelderly person enrolled in Medicaid in a given state in thousands.

UNINSURED: The percent of the population not covered by insurance within a state as a measure of the potential Medicaid population of the state.

PHYSICIAN: The number of physicians (in thousands) in a state used as a control for physician induced demand.

PER DIEM: The prevailing per diem health care charge by state, as a control for the overall cost of medical care.

PID HOUSE: The ratio of Democrats in the lower house of the state legislature.

PID SENATE: The ratio of Democrats in the upper house of the state legislature. (For Nebraska I used county presidential voting data as a proxy.)

EDUCATION: The percent of state residents with a high school diploma, used as a control variable.

INCOME: Average per capita income of state residents used as a control for Medicaid expenditures given that a 1995 GAO report concludes that states with higher average per capita incomes spend more on Medicaid.

Table 2: Logistic Regression Coefficients ADOPT as Dependent Variable

	ß	s.e.
NEIGHBORS	0.9430*	0.4890
MEDICAID ENROLLEES	0.0003*	0.0001
MEDICAID EXPENSES	0.0012**	0.0003
UNINSURED	0.0418	0.0352
PHYSICIAN	0.0173**	0.0026
PER DIEM	0.0002	0.0003
PID HOUSE	0.0002	0.0210
PID SENATE	0.0030	0.0214
EDUCATION	-0.0366	0.0269
INCOME	-0.0964	0.0686
CONSTANT	0.9706	2.7589

-2 Log Likelihood = 209.200
Chi-Square = 228.209 24df
Percent Improvement = 91.2
N = 750

*$p<.05$; **$p<.001$

Note: Coefficients for dummy variables using Stimson's method are not reported.

Data and Methods
I collected 750 observations, 50 states over 15 years (1982 to 1996) and performed a logistic regression on the cross-sectional pooled time series data. I used Stimson's correction to control for the autocorrelation.[1] The results are reported in table 2.

As expected, NEIGHBOR, MEDICAID ENROLLEES, and MEDICAID EXPENSE all had statistically significant coefficients in the predicted direction. The geographical variable NEIGHBOR has the largest single coefficient, thus the presence of a neighboring state that has or has applied for a waiver greatly influences the probability that the state in question will adopt a waiver. Second to that, the two Medicaid variables, while small, have similar effects, given that the actual value taken on by these variables is fairly large.

A surprising finding is that the variable meant to control for physician-induced demand is highly significant. Thus, it would appear that the number of physicians in the population increases the likelihood that a state will adopt a managed care arrangement for the provision of Medicaid.

Discussion
Overall, logit coefficients say little on their own. Instead, interesting interpretations result from transforming the coefficients into probabilities and examining how these probabilities change as the values of the variables change. In table 3, I present a simple examination of how the probability of adopting a managed care approach to Medicare changes when a neighboring state has such a program, varying the values for MEDICAID EXPENSE and MEDICAID ENROLLEES while keeping all other variables at their mean.

Table 3: Predicted Probability of Adoption Varying the Value of Key Variables

NEIGHBOR	MEDICAID ENROLLEES (in thousands)	MEDICAID EXPENSE (in thousands)	PREDICTED PROB-ABILITY
Yes	30	$828.00	79%
Yes	702	$2,712.00	98%
Yes	7,289	$6,001.00	99%
No	30	$828.00	59%
No	702	$2,712.00	94%
No	7,289	$6,001.00	99%

As table 3 shows, in situations where one would expect a state to refrain from adopting a managed care approach, when both expenses and enrollees are low, the presence of such a plan in a neighboring state increases the probability of adoption by 20 percent (59 percent versus 79 percent). However, as both the number of enrollees and the amount of expenses grow large, the impact of a neighboring state diminishes, with only a 4 percent difference at the mean and no difference at the maximum values. Specifically, in a state with a Medicaid population of 30,000 and per capita Medicaid expenses of $828, that is surrounded by states that are not pursuing Section 1115 waivers, there is a 59 percent chance that the state will begin a Section 1115 demonstration project. However, as Medicaid population and expenses increase to the average, 702,000 enrollees and $2,712 per capita expenditures, the likelihood, even in the absence of an innovative neighbor, is 94 percent that the state will begin a Section 1115 demonstration project. Thus, as one would expect, when internal financial incentives are present, a state will pioneer, but when there is no such incentive, a state will adopt policy innovations when they observe them in neighboring states. This is much as the innovation diffusion literature predicts.

This chapter supports the notion that when there is a need to control cost, states develop innovative policies to achieve that goal. That is, when budgetary pressure is present, states will innovate to develop a solution to the problem of balancing cost containment while providing health care to the indigent and the elderly in long-term care. Further, it shows that in the absence of pressure to innovate, states will adopt policies enacted in neighboring states that have reduced costs. Overall, it seems that cost containment has become a driving force in state-based health care policy innovation. In the next section I examine a federal attempt to balance the three competing goals, cost containment, quality, and access by looking at the Federal Employees Health Benefits Plan and its use of a regulated market to achieve these goals.

Summary and Conclusions
As table 1 and graph 1 showed, health care costs have been increasing at an increasing rate since the early 1960s. Throughout this period, there were attempts to control costs at the federal level through the introduction of the Resource Based Relative Value Scale (RBRVS) for physician charges and the Diagnostic Related Groups (DRG) plan for hospital coverage. These were attempts to control the price factor of the cost function, (Price) x (Quantity) = Costs for medical care. This chapter examined how states innovated their Medicaid programs, for which they share responsibility with the federal government, to adapt to changing economic factors present in health care through the past three decades.

The first state to truly innovate was Arizona. In 1982, using the waiver provisions under Section 1115, the state developed the Arizona

Health Care Cost Containment System (AHCCCS). AHCCCS was designed to tackle the other component of the cost function for medical care, quantity of services. Through the use of health maintenance organizations, the state would be able to control the quantity of services provided and thereby reduce overall costs. Arizona's program was soon viewed as a model for other states and was rapidly imitated.

The policy innovation begun by Arizona quickly spread across the country due to the Clinton administration's willingness to provide Section 1115 waivers. This proceeded much as Schneider and Teske with Mintrom note, "like ripples created by dropping a stone in a pond . . . " (1995, 221). However, the pattern of innovation diffusion is unique in this case because it advanced in an entrepreneurial fashion driven by economic incentives at the state level, but with the assistance of the federal government. While the classic literature indicates that the presence of a pioneering neighbor should impact the adoption decision of a state, in this case, the presence of an innovative neighbor does in fact have a major impact on whether a particular state will pursue Medicaid change through Section 1115. Nonetheless, there is also strong evidence that economic factors provided an incentive for a state to pursue cost-saving Medicaid policy change. Generally, states with higher Medicaid costs per enrollee and greater Medicaid eligible populations were more likely to pursue cost-saving innovations like AHCCCS, regardless of what neighboring states were doing. In fact, the states pursuing innovations for cost savings were the driving force behind the early implementations of Section 1115 waiver programs. In this sense, the innovation diffusion that is present in the spread of Section 1115 waivers can also be viewed as an intergovernmental entrepreneurial movement like that described by Schneider and Teske with Mintrom who describe a system in which the states themselves are the entrepreneurs within a federalist system:

> There is a clear intergovernmental dimension to the diffusion of innovation. Americans have a long-standing propensity to tinker with the way in which public services are delivered . . . waves of reform have periodically swept across America's state capital and its myriad of local governments, changing patterns of service delivery. Many of these reforms are structured around a dialogue between the national government and local governments, with the federal government endorsing reforms developed in a small number of local areas and then fostering their widespread adoption. (1995, 221)

Section 1115 waivers present a unique opportunity to see a real-world example of the theory that Schneider et al. express in the passage above. The data presented in this chapter indicates that states are indeed flexible and sophisticated forms of government, able to innovate and adapt to changing circumstances. When the goal is to contain costs, states will develop new policies and new systems of delivery for state-provided services to achieve that purpose. States are also mimics, thus, when one state develops a better or cheaper way of providing services, a neighboring state is highly likely to follow suit. Thus, state government truly provides a policy laboratory where new and innovative methods of providing citizen services are developed, tested, and perfected. In the case of Section 1115 waivers, the entrepreneurial efforts by the states were driven by a desire to reduce Medicaid expenditures. The innovation was allowed to diffuse and indeed flourish because the federal government fostered it. Thus, Section 1115 waivers present an excellent example of the intergovernmental dimension of entrepreneurial innovation diffusion.

Bibliography

Aaron, Henry J., and William B. Schwartz. 1984. *The Painful Prescription: Rationing Hospital Care*. Washington, D.C.: The Brookings Institution.

Berry, Francis Stokes, and William D. Berry. 1992. "Tax Innovation in the States: Capitalizing on Political Opportunity." *American Journal of Political Science* 36 (3): 715-742.

Congressional Budget Office. 1993. *Trends in Health Spending: An Update*. Washington, D.C.: The Government Printing Office.

Davidson, Stephen D. 1980. *Medicaid Decisions: A Systematic Analysis of the Cost Problem*. Cambridge, Mass.: Ballinger Publishing

Downs, George. 1976. *Bureaucracy Innovation and Public Policy*. Lexington, Mass.: Lexington Books.

Feldstein, Paul J. 1993. *Health Care Economics: 4th Edition*. Albany: Delmar Publishers, Incorporated.

Gray, Virginia. 1973. "Innovations in the States: A Diffusion Study." *American Political Science Review* 67 (4): 1174-1185.

Grupp, Fred W., Jr., and Alan R. Richards. 1975. "Variations in Elite Perceptions of American States as Referents for Public Policy Making." *American Political Science Review* 69(3): 850-858.

Levit, Katharine R., Helen C. Lazenby, Lekha Sivarajan, Madie W. Stewart, Bradley R. Brader, Cathy A. Cowan, Carolyn S. Donham, Anna M. Long, Patricia A. McDonnell, Arthur L. Sensenig, Jean M. Stiller, and Darleen K. Won. 1994. "National Health Expenditures 1993." *Health Care Financing Review* 16(1): 247-294.

Menzel, David C., and Irwin Feller. 1977. "Leadership and Interaction Patterns in the Diffusion of Innovation among the American States." *Western Political Quarterly* 30(3): 528-536.

Schneider, Mark, and Paul Teske with Michael Mintrom. 1995. *Public Entrepreneurs: Agents for Change in American Government*. Princeton, N.J.: Princeton University Press.

Sigelman, Lee. 1980. "Gauging the Public Responses to Presidential Leadership." *Presidential Studies Quarterly* 10: 427-433.

Stevens, Robert, and Rose Mary Stevens. 1974. *Welfare Medicine in America: A Case Study of Medicaid.* New York: Free Press.

Stimson, James A. 1985. "Regression in Space and Time: A Statistical Essay." *American Journal of Political Science* 29 (3): 915-947.

United States Bureau of the Census. 2001. *The United States Census.* Washington, D. C.: The Government Printing Office.

Walker, Jack. 1969. "The Diffusion of Innovations among the American States." *American Political Science Review* 63 (3): 880-899.

Weimer, David L., and Aidan Vining. 1992. *Policy Analysis Concepts and Practice, Second Edition.* Englewood Cliffs, N.J.: Prentice Hall.

Weissert, Carol, and William Weissert. 1996. *Governing Health: The Politics of Health Policy.* Baltimore, M.D.: The Johns Hopkins University Press.

Chapter 4

Lawrence J. Grossback

Policy Innovation and Reinvention in an Intergovernmental Context: Minnesota's Approach to State Mandates on Local Governments

Introduction

According to most measures, Minnesota is an innovative state. The reputation is both accurate and to be expected. The reputation is expected because Minnesota ranks high on most of the characteristics we associate with innovative states. It is a relatively wealthy state, its citizens tax themselves at a high rate, the government spends at a high rate, and its citizens have traditionally seen an active and innovative government as a legitimate and worthwhile enterprise. (This is showing signs of change as evidenced by the increasing strength of the Republican Party and the election of the libertarian leaning Independence Party Governor Jesse Ventura.) Minnesota's accomplishments in government innovation are many. It ranks fourth in the number of Innovations in American Government Awards (with a total of seven) (Institute for Government Innovation 2000). It was the first to ban smoking in restaurants, the first to allow children choice among public schools, and was a leader in implementing charter schools, guaranteeing health care, and in suing tobacco companies (Elazar, Gray, and Spano 1999). It is the only state with a

government body, the Board of Government Innovation and Cooperation, whose mission is to foster local government innovation. Combined,
these factors paint a picture of a state government that works.

The policy addressed in this case study, however, is not a clear-cut
success. It is not even a study of one of Minnesota's innovations. In fact,
it comes close to being a story of policy failure. The policy in question is
how states deal with the impact of state imposed mandates on local governments. Mandates, broadly defined, are laws or rules that tell lower
units of government what they must or must not do. Mandates include,
but are not limited to, requirements to provide specific programs, minimum policy standards, required administrative procedures, and restrictions on policy initiatives or revenue sources. Intergovernmental mandates are an issue because they raise questions about the most appropriate level of government for setting, implementing, and funding policies
(Office of Legislative Auditor 2000). Minnesota's policies designed to
deal with this issue come close to failure because after nearly two decades of studies, commission reports, and laws, local governments remain
troubled by the impact of mandates and the issue continues to be a primary source of tension in state-local relations.

Minnesota's lack of success in dealing with this issue is something
of a puzzle. We could reasonable expect that a good government state
with a history of innovative policies could pioneer a new approach to this
perpetual issue. While this puzzle might plague Minnesota's policy makers, it is of some help to those interested in understanding policy innovation and change at the state and local level. Puzzles are often the source
of good stories and good research. This puzzle allows us to address a
number of important questions. If Minnesota has not produced any truly
innovative policies related to mandates, it has reinvented several policies
pioneered by other states. Reinvention, or the modification of core innovations, is a key process that often characterizes controversial policies
that continually reappear on a state's agenda (Glick and Hays 1991). This
study uses the mandate issue to address a number of questions within the
policy reinvention and innovation literature. What has led Minnesota to a
near continuous interest in mandates? What factors drive a state to reinvent a policy and how well do they explain Minnesota's experiences?
What factors influenced the success or failure of Minnesota's reinventions? Finally, this case allows us to address these questions in the
unique circumstances of a policy that directly addresses intergovernmental relations. What challenges does the intergovernmental nature of
the mandate issue pose for the successful development and implementa-

tion of innovative policies? Finally, by focusing in on a single state's actions over time we can identify additional influences that might need to be included in our theories of innovation or reinvention (Hays 1996).

Policy Reinvention and Policy Change

The policy innovation literature has traditionally focused on questions such as what characteristics produce variations in a state's willingness to innovate or what makes a state willing to adopt a certain policy innovation (Nice 1994). Studies regarding the decision to adopt an innovation often asked the questions of when in the process of diffusion might a state adopt a policy or to what extent would they adopt a particular innovation. The second question took scholars beyond the adoption question to ask whether certain characteristics might help explain why a state adopted all or only parts of a recent innovation (Glick and Hays 1991). Closely related to this issue is the concept of policy reinvention. Reinvention captures the idea that a policy is not likely to remain unchanged as it diffuses among the states. Glick and Hays note that the timing of an adoption is only one dimension of a state's innovativeness (Glick and Hays 1991:837). Late adopters, if they change the content of the policy, may be equally or more innovative than states that adopt a policy early on. The reinvention perspective links the diffusion of an idea to the evolving content of the policy and allows analysts to ask not just what led to an adoption but what led a state to make changes in the policy.

Henry Glick and Scott Hays have offered the most thorough treatment of the influences on reinvention during policy diffusion (Glick and Hays 1991; Hays 1996). They propose five influences on policy reinvention. The first is social learning, or, more simply put, time. States learn from the experiences of previous adopters and use that information to make policy changes. They further hypothesize that new policies will become more comprehensive over time as states learn more and have fewer reasons to act tentatively. A second factor influencing reinvention is the amount of controversy surrounding a policy. Hays argues that controversy is the one factor that might inhibit a policy from expanding as it diffuses (Hays 1996). Two aspects of a state's political environment are thought to influence reinvention. Hays theorizes that more professional states are often early adopters and more likely to adopt less comprehensive laws. Early adopters do not have the opportunity to learn from previous experiences and thus act in a more incremental fashion. Political support is also thought to affect reinvention. According to Hays, strong ideological or political party support is nearly a necessary condition for

the adoption or expansion of a controversial innovation. For less controversial innovations, professionalism and party support are likely to be
less influential. The final influence is societal need. Most models of the
policy making see new policies as a response to a need or problem in
society. Following this logic, Hays hypothesizes that with greater need
comes a more comprehensive law.

This leaves us with a model of policy reinvention that sees policy
changes as a function of social learning, legislative professionalism, ideology, and societal need. Studies of the diffusion of child abuse reporting
laws, crime victim compensation laws, living wills, and campaign finance reforms confirm many of the hypotheses. Hays finds that most
policies expand in scope over time, that less controversial laws expand
more quickly, that less professional legislatures often adopt more comprehensive laws, and that societal need is related to reinvention (Hays
1996). Party support does not appear to matter.

These findings are the result of a comparative study of all fifty states.
The question here is how well do they help us understand how an individual state adjusts a policy over time. As these factors change over time,
do they help explain how a state alters a policy? What influences on
policy change and reinvention might be missing? Does this theory need
to account for aspects of intergovernmental relations? The case of Minnesota's mandate policies is well suited to answer these questions. Minnesota is a highly professional state that has a strong tradition of local
governance and a very active intergovernmental lobby. By looking at the
history of Minnesota's attempts to deal with this issue we can see how
well the current theory of reinvention explains the policies Minnesota has
enacted and we may be able to identify other factors that need to be included. I begin with a brief description of the mandate issue. I then present Minnesota's approach to the mandate problem, highlighting the reinventions and innovations they enacted. Finally, I discuss the factors
that contributed to the policies enacted and their success or failure.

The Mandate Issue

Intergovernmental mandates raise questions about the appropriate level
of government for setting, implementing, and funding policies. Mandates
have traditionally been seen as a means of dealing with two problems:
the guarantee of individual rights and negative externalities. It has been
argued that mandates are an appropriate means of protecting government
services or individual rights that should be available to citizens regardless of where they reside. Externalities are a concern because of the in-

stances where negative effects of either public or private activities cannot be contained within a given jurisdiction. Mandates can also be justified on the grounds that the state has a compelling interest in local affairs. A state government may need to ensure that the impact of local decisions on state finances is considered, or the state might want to ensure the proper functioning of local governments. This last argument is often used to support good government concerns such as open meeting laws, ethical practices for local government officials, and data access provisions.

Mandates would not be an issue if there were only arguments in favor of their use. Mandates are criticized for four main reasons (Office of the Legislative Auditor 2000). First, mandates often preempt local authority and restrict the ability of local officials to respond to local conditions. The preemption of local control raises a second issue, accountability. Mandates often obscure the lines of accountability by removing decisions from elected officials who have close contact with constituents. Third, mandate opponents argue that one-size-fits-all policies rarely achieve their objective in an efficient or effective manner. Mandates can ignore local variations in policy problems and the capacity of local units of government to respond to them. Mandates might also inhibit innovative responses to a policy problem by reducing the number of decision makers involved in a problem. Finally, we come to the most vocal criticism, cost. A prominent aspect of the mandate debate is the impact of underfunded or unfunded mandates on state and local budgets. The United States Advisory Commission on Intergovernmental Relations summed up the debate well, noting, "Much of the mandate controversy surrounds the mismatch between mandated responsibilities and local funding capacities" (Advisory Commission on Intergovernmental Relations 1990).

Cost studies commissioned by the U.S. Conference of Mayors, the National Association of Counties, and the National League of Cities focused attention on the fiscal impact of state imposed mandates. Local governments were found to suffer from the combined impact of having to spend money according to state guidelines while having their taxing authority restricted (Kelly 1993). Local government groups responded by pursuing relief from unfunded mandates through cost reimbursement mechanisms, constitutional amendments to require state funding of mandates, and the removal of noncompliance penalties when state funding was absent (Kelly 1994). Twenty-four states enacted general statutory or constitutional funding provisions (Zimmerman 1995). The provisions have seldom had the desired affect (Office of the Legislative Auditor

2000). Janet Kelly found that states' legislatures often bypassed the funding mechanisms when enacting costly mandates (Kelly 1994).

Kelly attributed the spotty success of the reimbursement provisions to a lack of legislative commitment, difficulties in accurately estimating the cost of a given mandate, and the tendency to focus on administrative compliance burdens over cost issues (Kelly 1994). In response to these findings, analysts turned their attention to alternative means of developing cost estimates as well as to broader approaches to the mandate problem. Scholars suggested a solution based on improved intergovernmental communication. Kelly found that some states with weak funding provisions had few unfunded mandates due to a history of good intergovernmental relations. Among the lessons drawn from Kelly's research was that an excessive focus on cost issues had hindered the development of policies or relationships that might have addressed the broader issues of local autonomy and the division of government services.

Kelly called for a "partnership" approach to intergovernmental policy making that stopped treating mandates as a side issue of the fiscal burdens on local government (Kelly 1993). The partnership approach is characterized by a movement away from institutional solutions to the cost problem and toward a dialogue between levels of government that allow each side to see their common goals and the variations in their constituent's policy priorities. This approach suggests the use of local government networks to develop cost estimates, periodic reviews of mandates initiated by local governments, explanations that provide a clear rationale for the mandate and of the appropriate role for each level of government, and mechanisms that would foster improved communication between state and local government officials (Zimmerman 1995).

The Minnesota Approach to Mandates

Minnesota presents a unique setting for the study of mandates. The state has a strong tradition of active state and local governance and a long history of addressing mandate concerns. Minnesota's political culture has traditionally supported community provision of goods and services and paved the way for cities and counties to aggressively work to improve their citizens' standard of living (Elazar, Gray, and Spano 1999). This tradition has resulted in a sensitive pattern of state-local relations. The relationship has not always approached a level of "Minnesota nice" often associated with the state. The relationship has become strained as state programs and finances have come to dominate. The strain is exacerbated by the combination of state restrictions on local revenue sources and a wide variety of state requirements for service delivery. Officials in Minnesota enacted a number of policies to address the mandate issue; policies that look much like the partnership approach described above (Office of the Legislative Auditor 2000). Several of these policies are adoptions of other states' innovations, a few involve the reinventing of a policy idea, and one is an innovative way to address mandate concerns.

Reinvention in Minnesota's Mandate Policies

A study by Minnesota's Office of the Legislative Auditor documented the state's near continuous interest in the mandate issue (Office of the Legislative Auditor 2000). Minnesota first addressed the issue in a conventional way, requiring fiscal notes for mandates' on local governments and a number of other special governing districts. Fiscal notes provide a cost estimate of individual mandates and are designed to provide state lawmakers with a reliable estimate of a mandates' fiscal impact. Fiscal notes are designed to ensure that local government concerns over cost are taken into account during the consideration of a mandate. Counter to the expectations of the innovation and reinvention literatures, Minnesota was late to adopt the use of fiscal notes and when it did, it adopted a less comprehensive law. Three factors limit the application of Minnesota's fiscal note procedures. Minnesota's statute allows only the chair and ranking minority members of the tax committees in each legislative chamber to request a fiscal note. Also, local fiscal impact notes are generally limited to proposals that would entail at least one million dollars in implementation costs; this reduces the applicability of the law to many procedural or administrative requirements that do not entail high implementation costs (Office of the Legislative Auditor 2000:43). Finally, Minnesota's statute lists thirteen exemptions from fiscal notes, many of which allow the state to impose fiscal and administrative burdens on local governments.

Minnesota did make several important adjustments to the fiscal note process. In line with the role of social learning in the reinvention literature, the adjustments were made in reaction to lessons learned from previous states. Studies of existing fiscal note procedures found that the notes were often qualitative in nature and, did not provide real cost estimates, and that they were often inaccurate (Kelly 1993). The inaccuracies were attributed to the lack of local government involvement in cost estimation. Minnesota's procedures address two of these concerns, requiring quantitative estimates of implementation costs and using a network of local governments to assist in developing the estimate. A third change involved the adoptions of guidelines that set a goal of ten days for the completion of the estimates. This change was an attempt to ensure that the information would be made available in time to inform the policy discussion that led to the request for a fiscal note.

Several factors have hindered the ability of Minnesota's fiscal note to help reduce local government concerns over the costs associated with state-imposed mandates. The first constraint is the limited applicability of the law. The requirement that requests come only from ranking members of the tax committees reduces the number of legislators likely to make use of the instruments and a large list of exemptions reduces its over all impact. A second limiting factor is that some costs of the reviews are deducted from county and city aid (Office of the Legislative Auditor 2000). This likely reduces the willingness of local governments to request fiscal notes. Finally, a review by the Minnesota Legislative Auditor found that the process is not well implemented. The auditor's report found that few fiscal notes are completed, those that are, are usually at the request of local government associations, and they are often completed late in the legislative session when the information is less likely to be of use (Office of the Legislative Auditor 2000:44). While this example illustrates that learning can produce policy reinventions, it also demonstrates that reinvention is not a sufficient condition for successful implementation.

The second conventional mandate policy adopted was a reimbursement statute that allows local governments to suspend implementation of a mandate if state funding falls below 85 percent of the statewide cost of implementation. Again, counter to expectations, Minnesota was late in adopting this law and adopted among the most restrictive reimbursement provisions in the country. As of 1998 at least twenty-four states had adopted some form of reimbursement procedure, some as early as 1979. Many of these procedures go well beyond Minnesota's, often requiring full state funding or that the state pay for significant portions of all mandate costs, not just those designated by the legislature (Zimmerman 1995). Minnesota's reimbursement law is restrictive in that it requires the legislature to make specific reference to the statute in order to designate a mandate as being subject to this provision; to date no such designation has been made.

Minnesota's late adoption of a limited reimbursement provision is something of a puzzle. First, Minnesota does not appear to have expanded upon the experiences of other states. There is little evidence Minnesota used existing information from studies that showed that more comprehensive constitutional reimbursement provisions were a more effective means to control mandate costs (Kelly 1995). Other studies question the overall effectiveness of reimbursement policies, but they tend to measure success in terms of the savings to local governments or the reduction in the number of mandates. These indicators of success are those associated with local government units and may not fully account for the interest of state government. This raises an important point as to why Minnesota enacted such a limited statute. There may have been significant disagreement over whether there was a societal need or policy problem that had to be addressed. This may rescue existing explanations of policy reinvention. The Minnesota legislature has often expressed some skepticism of the burden of mandates. In an important way this may make mandate policies such as fiscal notes and reimbursement provisions something of a controversial policy; a controversy that pits local governments against state policy-makers. While not a classic definition of controversy, this does raise an important role for problem definition that current theories might miss. If state leaders do not see mandates as a problem, then local government concerns may be brushed aside with inaction or placated with a restrictive policy.

Around the time that fiscal notes and mandate reimbursement provisions were enacted, Minnesota put in place a third mandate related tool, mandate explanations. The policy of requiring a statement of legislative intent or state interest has been advocated since at least 1990 when the now defunct American Commission of Intergovernmental Relations listed it as part of a model state policy (Advisory Commission on Intergovernmental Relations 1990). As enacted, Minnesota's mandate explanations added significantly to the existing policy by requiring that all new mandates be accompanied by an explanation that described the goals of the mandate, how performance standards were designed to allow for local government flexibility, how the mandate would be paid for, and efforts at involving local governments in the design of the mandate. The required elements of the explanations were an attempt to increase the dialogue between state legislators, agency staff, and local government officials. The explanations did not have the desired affect. In 1998 the law was changed to make the explanations optional. Mandate explanations now have to be requested by the chair or ranking member of the committee hearing the bill that contains the mandate. More importantly, a review by the legislative auditor found no evidence that a single explanation has been requested (Office of the Legislative Auditor 2000:49). When asked, the staffs of key legislative committees were often unaware that the explanations existed. We can now see a pattern emerging. Minnesota belatedly followed the lead of early innovators, but had little success implementing the policy. In this instance an important reinvention withered on the vine due to a lack of commitment from the legislature and a lack of knowledge among staff that might make use of the policy tool. We have reason to believe that this policy might help address local government concerns because a 1999 survey of Minnesota's local governments revealed that 89 percent of the respondents agreed or strongly agreed with the idea that the state should provide a clear statement of the rationale for enacting a mandate (Office of the Legislative Auditor 2000).

Innovation in Minnesota's Mandate Policies

Minnesota has employed one innovation in an effort to address the mandate issue, the Board of Government Innovation and Cooperation (henceforth the BGIC or the Board). The BGIC implements several programs designed to improve the quality and efficiency of local government services and to provide incentives for innovation and cooperation. The Board fosters innovation by helping to remove financial barriers and state requirements (Minnesota Board of Government Innovation and Cooperation 2001). The BGIC originated in a study group convened by a prominent Minnesota policy organization, the Citizen's League. The Citizen's League study commission of local government services recommended that local governments be allowed to focus on achieving results rather than on following state procedures (Wilson 2000). In order to facilitate this, the legislature gave the BGIC the authority to grant waivers and exemptions from a variety of administrative and procedural mandates when local governments have a plan for achieving the same or a better outcome. In addition to the waivers, the BGIC awards grants to support the development and implementation of innovative public services and works to facilitate mergers and cooperative efforts between local governments. Minnesota is currently the only state with an agency empowered to issue such waivers (Wilson 2000).

According to one of the directors of the original study, the purpose of the Board was to provide a means to move innovations into standard practice (Wilson 2000). The Board does this by assuming some of the financial risk associated with new service programs and by removing existing mandates that prevent innovative policies. Waivers from state laws and rules are the Board's primary tools to help address the impact of mandates. The waivers are, however, temporary. Rule waivers can last from two to four years; waivers from laws expire at the end of the legislative session held the year after the waiver was granted unless the legislature extends the waiver or makes a permanent change in the law (Office of the Legislative Auditor 2000:52). The BGIC has one additional power that is related to the mandate problem. The Board can make recommendations to the legislature regarding the elimination of state mandates that inhibit the provisions of efficient local services (Office of the Legislative Auditor 2000:53). These recommendations are designed to be a mechanism by which successful waivers or innovations can be applied statewide.

The actions of the BGIC have met with mixed reviews. The Board was named one of twenty-five finalists for the 2000 Innovations in American Government Awards, a designation that brings with it a $20,000 grant (Schroeder 2000). In announcing the award, the sponsors cited the Board's ability to contribute to more efficient and effective services by removing bureaucratic barriers to the implementation of new ideas (Innovations in American Government Awards Program 2000). The Board has not always received such strong support. The current and previous governor have recommended terminating the agency as a means of recouping savings from the Board's one-million-dollar budget. The Board survived both attempts due to support in the Minnesota legislature. The grant program that seeks to foster cooperative or innovative policies tends to receive the most praise; the waiver program that can help address mandate concerns has produced little activity in recent years.

The study by the Minnesota Legislative Auditor found that few local governments have applied for waivers from laws or rules. The number of waiver applications has dropped from a high of twenty-three in the first year of operations to only one in each of 1998 and 1999 (Office of the Legislative Auditor 2000:53). This is something of a surprise given that Minnesota's local governments were most critical of mandates that affected administrative procedures, those the Board has explicit powers to waive. The Board has also made few recommendations regarding the elimination of mandates. The Board's past director did not take the lead on recommending policy changes, mainly because the Board did not have the staff or resources to study the recommendations (Office of the Legislative Auditor 2000). The director noted that he has provided testimony in support of successful projects. Despite these limited actions, the auditor was able to find nine changes to Minnesota laws or rules that were associated with waivers granted by the BGIC. If we are to understand why Minnesota's efforts at addressing the mandate issue through innovative or reinvented policies did or did not succeed, we need to look at the possible reasons behind the waning of the waiver program.

The Board's meager resources are part of the explanation. The Board has only two staff members and has a budget of close to one million dollars, half of which is slotted for grants to local governments. The Board's director cited resources as the main reason why the Board has not undertaken studies of state mandates. The limited resources are strongly related to the Board's lack of strong political support. Republican lawmakers and recent governors have not been supportive of the agency, often making the argument that other resources are available to accomplish the Board's goals (Government Innovation: Deservedly, Minnesota Scores High 2000). The Board's director also offered several reasons for the decline in waiver applications (Office of the Legislative Auditor 2000). He suggested that the strong economy of the last decade had reduced the pressure on local governments to increase efficiencies as a means to save money or to implement new services. He also acknowledged that state agencies had become more willing to work with local governments, so it was less likely that the local governments would bypass the agency and seek a waiver from the Board. Finally, he noted that the Board can only waive required processes and not outcomes, and that this might limit its applicability.

Many local government officials noted the limited scope of the Board's authority. The legislative auditor surveyed local governments as to why they had not applied to the Board or what improvements they would suggest for how the Board operates. The majority of respondents failed to answer the question or stated that they had not yet needed a waiver, especially small cities and townships. A large number of the respondents were unaware of the Board's powers, this despite annual mailings by the Board. More specific concerns did emerge from the responses of county governments and large cities. Almost a third of the large city and a half of county officials indicated problems with a cumbersome application procedure, the limited authority of the Board, and the temporary nature of the waivers. Often the low probability of success was mentioned in conjunction with the local governments' lack of resources to commit to the application process. In general, local government officials suggested the Board receive more resources, that they simplify and speed up the waiver process, and that the legislature allow the Board greater authority to waive laws and to make the changes permanent (Office of the Legislative Auditor 2000) (data from a survey of local governments). It is important to note the Board has worked to re-

duce the length of its applications and to publicize its efforts through annual mailings to local government administrators. Given the results of
the survey, these efforts do not appear to have helped to improve the operation of the waiver program or its ability to mitigate the concerns local
governments have regarding mandates. In this instance we see a lack of
political support, a lack of resources for implementation, poor communication, and outside factors such as the economy combining to reduce the
effectiveness of this policy innovation. The task now is to combine these
findings with the earlier review of Minnesota's attempts to reinvent or
adjust existing policies to draw some lessons for our understanding of
policy change.

Factors Influencing Minnesota's Reinventions and Innovations
Having reviewed Minnesota's efforts in dealing with the mandate issue,
it is appropriate to look back to see how well they can inform our broader
understanding of policy reinvention and change. Current theories model
policy reinvention as a function of learning, controversy, societal need,
legislative professionalism, and political support. How well does Minnesota's experiences conform to this model? Are changes or additions to
our general ideas warranted? It appears they may be. Several lessons can
be drawn from this case study. Before presenting them, a note of caution
is in order. These lessons come from a single case looking at a single
policy in a single state; generalizations are thus to be taken lightly. The
value of in-depth case studies is that they can often help build new theories by offering important insight and details on how variables influence
the phenomenon of interest, and that we can do.

One clear lesson is that Minnesota did not entirely live up to its
reputation as an innovator, nor did it confirm to previous expectations
regarding the influence of learning and the existence of a professional
legislature. In two instances where Minnesota adopted existing innovations, they were late in adopting them, despite their level of professionalism, and the policies they enacted were not more comprehensive despite the lateness. Moreover, they did not always take into account previous experiences. Some lessons were learned and policies reinvented accordingly, such as with the changes to Minnesota's fiscal note procedures that required quantitative information, the use of a local government cost estimation network, and timely completion of reports. The lesson here may be that the impact of professionalism on the timing of
adoption and the impact of learning on the nature of the reinvention is
conditional on other variables. More professional states may do a better

job avoiding policy problems and thus be less likely to act early if a new policy innovation presents itself.

Societal need and controversy appear to be factors which condition the influence of professionalism and learning, but these too need clarification. Determining if there is a policy problem or societal need may not be as straightforward as previous research has suggested. In the case of Minnesota's mandate policies, the state legislature and local governments disagreed over whether a problem existed, and this mitigated the legislature's interest in adopting more comprehensive mandate relief policies. Problem definition might be a necessary addition to the theory of policy reinvention. Local governments defined the mandate problem as one of a lack of inclusion in policy development and of fiscal stress, whereas the legislature appears to have viewed it more as one of meeting the specific needs of individual local governments as they attempt to implement specific laws. The lack of agreement over how the problem should be defined appears to have precluded a consensus on the extent of the state's need for a more comprehensive policy.

Problem definition also stands apart from controversy. Controversy implies conflict, and that may not be the same as a lack of clear understanding as to the nature of the problem at hand. Hays argued that controversy would produce less comprehensive policies as states muddled their way through the political problems associated with a given case of reinvention. The nature of a reinvention and its comprehensiveness may well be limited by disagreement over the nature of a problem and the desire to retain control over existing policies. The role of problem definition is likely exacerbated by the intergovernmental nature of the mandate issue. Societal need, problem definition, and the lessons from other states differ by the level of government one works for or represents. In this instance it is the views of the state policy makers that truly matter. Disagreement between the levels of government may not reach the level of a true controversy, but it might restrain the expansion of a policy when adopted later in the life cycle of an innovation.

The concept of societal need also requires further clarification. Previous studies imply a single policy problem that a reinvented policy might help to cure and that the extent of this problem will influence the scope of the reinvention. However, numerous problem indicators may affect policy adoption and change. One factor that may need specific inclusion is the economy and the attendant fiscal impact on government finances. As Hays noted, recent studies have offered ambiguous conclusions about the impact of economic factors in state politics (Hays 1996).

The economy and fiscal stress played a key role in the adoption of new mandate policies in Minnesota and in the effectiveness of their innovations. As is the case with mandates more generally, the cost to local governments in terms of required programs and restricted revenue sources prompted many of the calls for change from local government officials and their lobbying associations. While the strong economy of the last decade may have reduced the fiscal stress associated with simultaneously meeting local demands and state mandates, the problem might worsen if an economic downturn reduced the ability of local governments to collect revenue while also reducing state aid. The economy also appears to have influenced the implementation of Minnesota's key mandate innovation, the waiver program of the Board of Government Innovation and Cooperation. The Board's director believed that the strong economy had reduced the fiscal stress on local governments and had resulted in fewer requests for waivers from state rules.

One final element may be missing from existing views on reinvention. The policy innovation literature has recently highlighted the role played by policy entrepreneurs. Mintrom has carefully documented the role of policy entrepreneurs in the diffusion of innovations in education policy (Mintrom 1997). This finding needs to be explored in the context of reinvention as well. Several entrepreneurs, both individuals and organizations, played a role in the shaping of Minnesota's mandate policies. The organizations that represent Minnesota's local governments played a key role in keeping the mandate issue on the agenda. The intergovernmental lobby is a powerful force in policy making both nationally and in Minnesota. A coalition of local government associations operates a mandate task force and lobbying effort that played a role in the adoption of many of these policies and in the call for a recent study by the legislative auditor. Equally important was the role of the Citizen's League in the creation of the BGIC. Their call for more flexibility in the implementation of state rules led several legislators to champion the Board and the ideas behind it.

Overall, existing theories of reinvention provide a strong base to help us understand how policies might change as they diffuse through the states. In the case of Minnesota's adoption of mandate policies we do see the influence of earlier states, policy need, and a unique form of controversy, but we also see the need to better account for issues related to problem definition, economic influences, and the political struggles that come not just with party politics but also the politics of intergovernmental relations.

Implementation, Policy Success, and Policy Change
While such an in-depth case study may not allow us to offer strong generalizations for policy reinvention, it is also well suited to address another question in the innovation literature, that of the success or failure of innovations. Four factors appear to have influenced the relative success or failure of Minnesota's mandate policies: recent policy experiences, the commitment of state officials, awareness of existing policies, and the availability of resources. Perhaps the only clear success among Minnesota's mandate policies is the fiscal note process that successfully incorporated research on the effectiveness of existing policies. The inclusion of quantitative measures of mandate cost, the use of local governments in developing cost estimation methods, and the quick completion of estimates have contributed to positive evaluations of the program. The majority of county and large-city officials surveyed by the Minnesota legislative auditor thought that the fiscal notes produced accurate and helpful information that was used by the legislature when considering proposed mandates (Office of the Legislative Auditor 2000).

The fiscal note process also helps to illustrate the importance of financial resources for successful implementation. The state's budget for fiscal notes was such that the Department of Finance was able to complete the studies as requested and in a timely fashion. A lack of resources can also inhibit effective implementation. The Board of Government Innovation and Cooperation was forced, in part, by a lack of resources to focus on grant making for policy innovations rather than on taking the lead in studying mandates in order to make recommendations for their removal from state law. As previously noted, local government officials supported the Board's activities and thought they should be given greater resources and more authority. The periodic review of mandates and the removal of those who no longer appear necessary have been included in a number of recommendations for state mandate policies (Advisory Commission on Intergovernmental Relations 1990). The BGIC appears to be a potential avenue for Minnesota to implement such a review, but the Board has been limited by its budget and has not been traditionally seen as a grant making body rather than as a tool for dealing with the broader mandate issue.

The lack of support for the activities of the BGIC is only one instance where the lack of commitment of state officials has hindered the implementation of Minnesota's mandate policies. The commitment of state officials and the awareness of existing policy tools go hand in hand.

The combined tools of the BGIC's waiver program, Minnesota's extensive mandate explanations, and even the limited reimbursement procedures offer an impressive opportunity to address the concerns of local governments, but the tools are seldom if ever used. The legislative auditor concluded that they could not offer a full evaluation of Minnesota's mandate policies or recommend policy changes because of the extent to which existing policies had not been used (Office of the Legislative Auditor 2000:61). That few people in state government were aware of the existence of mandate explanations is a sign of a lack of awareness of existing policy tools and a lack of commitment by the original sponsors of the policy. Despite having been on the books for nearly five years, neither the reimbursement policy nor the mandate explanations have been used. Clearly, a first step toward the successful implementation of an innovation or reinvention is to actually put the policy into use.

The Minnesota legislature has responded to local government concerns with potentially effective policies, but the unwillingness to use the policies has resulted in continued state-local tensions. Nowhere is this more evident than the study by the Minnesota's legislative auditor. Despite the enactment of the policies described in this review, strong majorities of county and city officials see the legislature and state agencies as unresponsive to their concerns regarding mandates (Office of the Legislative Auditor 2000). Mandates continue to be a source of concern for local governments and they continue to contribute to a strained state-local relationship. The failure of Minnesota's policies to address local government concerns resulted in a new round of complaints to the legislature and the call for the auditor's study. The adoption of new or altered policies does not ensure successful implementation, the question now is where will Minnesota's state government go following the auditor's report. To date the review has not resulted in any significant changes in policy or in the renewed commitment to existing policies. Apparently the commitment of the superior level of government is also critical when linking implementation to policy change.

The Obstacle of Intergovernmental Policy Making
Perhaps we should not be surprised that innovations and reinventions designed to address the mandate issue have had a difficult time succeeding. Intergovernmental relations are a difficult thing to manage. Altshuler and Behn go so far as to call federalism one of the dilemmas of innovation; a particularly difficult hurdle to overcome when fostering and implementing new policies (Altshuler and Behn 1997). They note that in-

novators and the policies they produce are constrained by the structures and organizations within which the innovation (or reinvention) must be adopted, implemented, and sustained. The decentralized and diverse federal system is among the most prominent structural aspects of American policy making. States may live up to their reputation as laboratories of democracy in terms of producing policy innovations and reinventions, but the ability to institutionalize those policies is often hindered by federalism. Intergovernmental policies often require the approval of superior levels of government, can require additional planning, and can make it difficult to know which innovations or experiments are most effective (Altshuler and Behn 1997).

These difficulties extend to the state level as well. Minnesota has 87 counties, 855 cities, 1,796 townships, 481 educational districts, 142 housing and redevelopment authorities, 22 port authorities, and 91 soil and conservation districts (Elazar, Gray, and Spano 1999:186). The counties range from rural areas of less than five thousand residents to highly urban counties of over one million residents. Minnesota's cities show a similar diversity, ranging in population from less than twenty to a combined 630,000 in the twin cities of Minneapolis and St. Paul. Together the respondents to the legislative auditor's survey identified close to 150 burdensome mandates. The diversity of local government responsibilities ensures they bring very different perspectives to the mandate problems. The burdens faced by large urban counties struggling to finance extensive human service policies is never going to equal the concerns of the small cities and towns that complained about state rules requiring them to leave polling stations open all day long. People in Minnesota like to vote and these small governments were perplexed that they had to remain open even after 100 percent of their eligible voters had cast their ballots, a very understandable concern. When we consider the needs of the state government to ensure minimum service standards, to ensure good government practices, and to oversee local government implementation of state programs, the situation becomes even more complex.

The complexity of intergovernmental issues brings us back to the factors influencing reinvention and innovation. Minnesota's experiences with reinventing mandate policies suggest that we need to engage in additional theorizing about what factors influence reinvention and policy change. I have already noted that problem definition and a more clearly defined concept of policy need might mitigate the influence of social learning and controversy, but we may need to recognize that all policies are not created equal. Scholars have offered a variety of policy typologies in an effort to account for the varying characteristics of public policies; perhaps this needs to be worked into our theories of policy change as well. Altshuler and Behn are correct to note the institutional challenges facing policy innovations. We may be able to account for the different paths of diffusion and the different influences on reinvention by taking better account of the variety of institutional constraints within which policies are adopted and implemented.

Finally, this study leaves us with several open questions. How do the characteristics of an issue affect the process of innovation and reinvention? What role do policy entrepreneurs play in the reinvention of innovations? What factors influence the development of a single state's policies over time? Hays first raised the issue of linking implementation to subsequent policy change. This issue remains to be addressed. The methods used here are a good start, but the lack of implementation of Minnesota's policies makes it difficult to draw any conclusions. Additional case studies that track a variety of issues over time may be needed to help us fully understand what helps some innovations succeed where others fail and how experiences with implementing policy innovations or reinventions are translated into policy change.

Bibliography

Advisory Commission on Intergovernmental Relations. 1990, September. *Mandates: Cases in State-Local Relations*. Washington, D.C.: Report M-173.

Altshuler, Alan A., and Robert D. Behn. 1997. "The Dilemmas of Innovation in American Government." *Innovations in American Government: Challenges, Opportunities, and Dilemmas*, eds. Alan A. Altshuler and Robert D. Behn, Washington, D.C.: The Brookings Institution 3-37.

Elazar, Daniel J., Virginia Gary, and Wyman Spano. 1999. *Minnesota Government and Politics*. Lincoln: University of Nebraska Press.

Glick, Henry R., and Scott P. Hays. 1991. "Innovation and Reinvention in State Policymaking: Theory and the Evolution of Living Will Laws," *Journal of Politics* 53 (August): 835-850.

Government Innovation; Deservedly, Minnesota Scores High," *Minneapolis Star Tribune*, 26 August 2000, sec. A, p. 16A.

Hays, Scott P. 1996a "The States and Policy Innovation Research: Lessons from the Past and Directions for the Future," *Policy Studies Journal* 24 no. (2): 321-326.

Hays, Scott P. 1996b. "Influences on Reinvention during the Diffusion Process," *Political Research Quarterly* 49 (September): 631-650.

Innovations in American Government Awards Program, "Minnesota Cuts Red
    Tape, Improves Services," 23 August 2000,
    http://www.ksg.harvard.edu/innovations/Finalists/2000/coop.htm (9 July
    2001).
Institute for Government Innovation. *Innovations in American Government.*
    http://www.ksg.harvard.edu/innovations/intro.htm (July 2000).
Kelly, Janet M. 1993. "A New Approach to an Old Problem: State Mandates,"
    Government Finance Review 9 (December): 27.
Kelly, Janet M. 1994. "Mandate Reimbursement Measures in the States,"
    American Review of Public Administration 24 (December): 351.
Kelly, Janet M. 1995. "Lessons from the States on Unfunded Mandates. Where
    There's a Will There's a Way," *National Civic Review* 84 (Spring) 133-9.
Minnesota Board of Government Innovation and Cooperation. "What Is the
    Board?" http://www.bgic.state.mn.us/board.html (8 July 2001).
Mintrom, Michael. 1997. "Policy Entrepreneurs and the Diffusion of Innova-
    tion," *American Journal of Political Science* 41 (July): 738-770.
Nice, David C. 1994. *Policy Innovation in State Government.* Ames: Iowa State
    University Press.
Office of the Legislative Auditor. 2000. *State Mandates on Local Governments.*
    St. Paul: State of Minnesota.
Schroeder, Dana. "Reichgott Junge Plans to Continue Policy Work from the
    Outside," *Minnesota Journal*, December 2000,
    http://www.citizensleague.net/mj/2000/12/junge.htm (8 July 2001).
Wilson, Kris Lyndon. "Two Minnesota Laws with League Ties Named Innova-
    tion Semifinalists," *Minnesota Journal*, July 2000,
    http://www.citizensleague.net/mj/2000/07/innovations.htm (8 July 2001).
Zimmerman, Joseph F. 1995. *State-Local Relations: A Partnership Approach.*
    West Port, Conn.: Praeger Press.

Chapter 5

Robert Stoker

Who Is Empowered?
Innovative Governance in Baltimore's Empowerment Zone

Policy is "a product of the struggle over a community's political arrangements" (Stone 1987, 17). The most basic policy problem urban leaders must confront is the problem of local governance, creating the capacity to act by coordinating the actions of numerous, diverse actors in common cause (Stone 1989). This chapter describes and discusses the governance scheme used in Baltimore, Maryland's empowerment zone (EZ). In Baltimore, a quasi-public corporation, Empower Baltimore Management Corporation (EBMC), was created to include numerous, diverse participants in empowerment zone governance. To organize the community and encourage its participation in the policymaking process EBMC has sponsored six community-based organizations called Village Centers. The Village Centers are an innovative form of community participation, but they are also a source of innovative programs to serve empowerment zone residents.

The empowerment zone initiative was designed to create sustainable change by activating local communities to influence the design and implementation of urban revitalization programs (HUD, 2000a). However, local communities are fragmented and many local stakeholders lack the social capital required to be effective participants in the policy making process. How local communities are organized and included in governance is a significant decision that creates opportunities and constraints for policy making. EBMC has mobilized the community by creating the Village Centers. This is an innovative solution to the problem of creating sustainable change because Baltimore has placed these new community-based institutions at the heart of the policy making process. Although performance has been uneven, several of the Village Centers have created innovative programs that integrate fragmented service systems to better serve empowerment zone residents.

Baltimore's Village Centers provide a source of hope for sustained activism in distressed communities. However, their creation has had consequences for the ways in which empowerment zone programs have been developed and implemented. The Village Centers shaped the distribution of program benefits throughout the empowerment zone in three ways. First, the role of the Village Centers varied depending upon the constituency being served. The Village Centers were critical links in the design and implementation of initiatives to assist zone residents. However, a professional staff housed within EBMC serviced business clients. Second, progress in making the Village Centers into viable organizations has been uneven; some Village Centers have become competent, active forces for change in their communities, others have languished. Not surprisingly, those communities that enjoyed more social capital in advance of the empowerment zone initiative have tended to organize more effectively to create Village Centers. This has had consequences for residents of the empowerment zone; some are well served by their Village Centers, and others are not. Third, the Village Centers have created a system of distributive politics within EBMC that has influenced the allocation of resources. Village Center participation in the governance process has resulted in a consistent pattern of resource distribution; the less-populated Village Centers have formed a coalition to distribute resources in a manner that disadvantages the most populous Village Centers.

The Empowerment Zones

The Omnibus Budget Reconciliation Act of 1993 authorized the Empowerment Zone/Enterprise Community initiative, including the creation of six urban and three rural empowerment zones. One hundred five communities of varying size throughout the United States were designated as empowerment zones or enterprise communities in the initial selection process completed in 1994 (HUD, 2000a). The six urban empowerment zones designated were located in Atlanta, Baltimore, Chicago, Detroit, New York, and Philadelphia/Camden. Urban empowerment zones are geographic areas within cities targeted for renewal through the use of a variety of tools including $100 million social services block grant, tax incentives, regulatory relief, and technical assistance. The initiative designated the Department of Housing and Urban Development (HUD) as the lead federal agency for the urban sites and emphasized the importance of mobilizing local communities to develop solutions to the problems of economic renewal and community revitalization.

"The Initiative recognizes that local communities, working together, can best identify and develop local solutions to the problems they face. The program provides performance-oriented, flexible Federal grant funding so communities can design local solutions that empower residents to participate in the revitalization of their neighborhoods." (HUD, 2000a)

Although the initiative emphasized local mobilization and resident participation, it did not specify how to mobilize or how to continue the momentum from the initial mobilization throughout the ten-year-long process of developing and implementing the program. Mobilization was a local problem and the initiative favored local solutions to local problems. However, HUD did create four key principles to guide the revitalization process (HUD, 2000b):

1. A strategic vision for change: what the community wants to become.
2. Community-based partnerships: encourage participation by all stakeholders.
3. Economic opportunity: creating jobs for zone residents, preparing zone residents for work, and assisting entrepreneurs so they can expand their businesses and create jobs.
4. Sustainable community development: comprehensive approaches to create livable and vibrant communities.

HUD's vision is that the empowerment zone/enterprise community initiative can plant the seeds of lasting, comprehensive change in distressed communities. However, because local stakeholders are more familiar with the constraints and opportunities that exist in local communities, the specific details of the program are left to local communities to decide. Local governing arrangements allow local communities to shape their opportunities and constraints.

Baltimore's Empowerment Zone

Baltimore's vision is to create "Neighborhoods of Choice" within its empowerment zone.[1] They hope to make zone neighborhoods desirable places to live and do business. Three principles have guided the development of Baltimore's program: to connect zone residents to the area's mainstream economy; to rebuild the social and neighborhood systems simultaneously and comprehensively; and to solve problems through grassroots mobilization of zone residents.

A nonprofit, quasi-public corporation, the Empower Baltimore Management Corporation (Empower Baltimore or EBMC), manages Baltimore's empowerment zone initiative. The mission of Empower Baltimore is "to foster sustained economic opportunities within the empowerment zone and to build communities in ways that give empowerment zone residents greater access to and readiness for those opportunities." A thirty-member board, most of whom are appointed by the mayor of Baltimore, directs EBMC. The board is composed of nine community representatives, one from each of the six Village Centers, one from Fairfield (an industrial area within the empowerment zone), and two from the Advisory Council; two representatives of the mayor; two appointees of the governor of Maryland; and seventeen appointed by the mayor from the business community, community institutions, foundations, and financial institutions participating in the EZ initiative.

The use of quasi-public corporations to manage redevelopment policy in Baltimore is commonplace. The primary organization that coordinates economic development policy in the city is corporate—the Baltimore Development Corporation. Other corporate organizations have influenced economic development in the city as well. Primary among these is Charles Center/Inner Harbor Management Incorporated, the corporation that coordinated the renewal of Charles Center (an office center in the downtown central business district) and redevelopment of the popular Inner Harbor attractions. Another example of the use of corporate management is the Baltimore Aquarium, Incorporated, which manages the National Aquarium in Baltimore (Stoker 1987).

The EBMC Board has a committee structure and staff. There are standing committees to design and oversee programs related to Baltimore's strategic plan. All initiatives developed by the committees pass through an executive committee composed of leading members of the board including the chairs of the standing committees. Meetings are open to the public and held at various locations around the city, normally in schools or places of worship. EBMC has established several standard patterns of doing business. With the exception of the Business Empowerment Center, an arm of EBMC that has a staff that provides outreach and services directly to business clients, EBMC is a contracting agency, not a direct provider of services. It is typical for EBMC staff to create program guidelines and requirements and then solicit bids for services from vendors. This allows EBMC to select qualified vendors and to contract for their services only for as long as they are needed. This reflects the philosophy of EBMC, which emphasizes performance and accountability, but views itself as a temporary organization. (EBMC was originally scheduled to go "out of business" after five years. However, that date has been delayed in part because of delays in developing viable Village Centers. The current projected sunset date for EBMC is the end of 2004.)

EBMC is also the liaison between the empowerment zone and city and state government. EBMC is represented on the mayor's subcabinet on the empowerment zone. The subcabinet group coordinates city agency actions with those of the empowerment zone. EBMC is also represented in state and local economic development agencies. The director of the Business Empowerment Center holds a seat on the State Department of Business and Economic Development Customer Management Task Force. (This represents the same sort of participation given to Maryland's primary political jurisdictions, the counties and Baltimore City.) Interagency coordination is carried out with numerous city agencies. Coordination on job placement has been achieved with the Office of Employment Development. Public safety initiatives have been designed and implemented in cooperation with the Baltimore City Police Department. Housing programs have been developed and managed with the cooperation of city housing officials. Baltimore Development Corporation (the local economic development authority) helped to design and manage business finance initiatives and the Fairfield industrial redevelopment plan.

Empower Baltimore has sponsored the creation of six Village Centers: East Harbor, Harlem Park, Historic East Baltimore Community Action Coalition (HEBCAC), Poppleton, Self-Motivated Community People, and Washington Village/Pigtown. Each is a separate, nonprofit, quasi-public corporation governed by its own board. The Village Centers are important components of EZ governance in matters such as social services, public safety, and job training because they are directly involved in planning and implementing initiatives related to these concerns. The Village Centers are less influential in matters pertaining to business service and finance. Although six Village Centers have been established, they vary in terms of their level of development and activity. All six Village Centers have completed the process for certification required by EBMC in order to represent the community and serve on the EBMC board and have signed "administrative agreements" with EBMC making them eligible to receive financial support.

EBMC's board has created an Advisory Council to advise them about policy matters. The Village Centers and representatives of other organizations in Baltimore are included on the Advisory Council. Half of the fifty-member Advisory Council is elected from the Village Centers. The other half is appointed by the mayor and includes representatives of foundations, city agencies, state agencies, and business and citizen advocacy groups. The Advisory Council meets monthly and is self-governing. Meetings of the Advisory Council are held "in the community" at public schools around the city. An elected chairperson runs the meetings according to an established agenda. Attention is paid to parliamentary procedure and minutes are recorded. Members of the Advisory Council know each other to some extent; however, sometimes participants are asked if they are, in fact, members of the Advisory Council and whom they claim to represent. The Advisory Council has experienced difficulty because many of its members fail to attend regularly. This became such a problem that the organization changed its bylaws to allow it to do business with fewer members present.

There is limited involvement of community groups outside the EZ in the governance structure. This is understandable given that the Village Centers —the primary vehicles for community participation—were organized based upon the geography of the EZ itself. The Village Centers have been encouraged to work with adjacent neighborhoods to solve problems such as trash collection. However, Village Center programs are closely monitored to assure that EZ funds are expended only to provide services to zone residents (a concern that reflects federal regulations). There are two exceptions to the pattern of limited community involvement from outside the empowerment zone. Some community groups are organized along geographic lines that are not completely within the EZ though substantial proportions of their geographic areas are (for example the Sandtown-Winchester neighborhood overlaps with the Self-Motivated Community People's Village Center and the Historic East Baltimore Community Action Coalition has organizational boundaries that overlap, but extend beyond the empowerment zone). When this situation arises, the awkwardness of fitting the existing EZ boundaries to the activities of existing community groups may result in some participation by community members from outside the zone or community groups not completely within the zone. The other exception is those members of the larger community of Baltimore who may be represented on the EBMC board or the Advisory Council.

Policy Implementation in Baltimore's Empowerment Zone
Policy implementation in Baltimore's empowerment zone runs along two very different tracks, one for businesses and another for zone residents. From the beginning, business clients have been served by a professional staff employed by Empower Baltimore. During the initial implementation of the zone programs these were workers detailed to the empowerment zone by various city agencies or quasi-public authorities. Later, a Business Empowerment Center (BEC) was created and staffed within EBMC. The effect of this was to insulate business clients and the programs that serve them from the long, arduous process of creating the Village Centers. Business clients who wanted training grants or financial assistance dealt with BEC staff or were referred to professional business redevelopment officials who work in partnership with the BEC.

While the separation of business services from resident services was doubtless an advantage to business clients, it has created problems in program coordination. Staff working for the BEC and its partners recruit businesses to relocate in the zone, resulting in the creation of job opportunities. However, in many instances, there are too few job-ready zone residents available to fill the new positions. Preparing the workforce to enter the job market is a function the Village Centers serve. With the exception of a small program oriented to custom train residents for job openings, there is little coordination between the BEC's business recruitment and job creation ventures and Village Center workforce initiatives.

Comparing Baltimore to Other Urban Empowerment Zones
In what ways is Baltimore's governance system like and unlike the other five original urban empowerment zones? A comparison of the governance structures of the six original urban empowerment zones concluded that Baltimore was similar to New York and Philadelphia/Camden; these empowerment zones have low to moderate integration with city govern-

ment and a two-tiered structure. Low to moderate integration means that zone policies are designed and implemented largely outside the formal structures of city government. The two-tiered structure means that there is one part of the governance structure that is concerned with zone-wide policy and another tier that influences and carries out zone activities on a neighborhood level (Nathan and Wright 1997).

Governance in all six empowerment zones emphasizes community participation. However, in comparison to other empowerment zones, Baltimore has sponsored more community-based organizations and given them more responsibility for delivering services to zone residents. In Atlanta's empowerment zone, the Atlanta Empowerment Zone Corporation (AEZC) is the primary policy making body. A board that is chaired by the mayor and includes local politicians, representatives of city agencies, corporate representatives, community representatives, and a representative of state government governs AZEC. AZEC has a staff that designs and implements programs in the zone. Although there is a Community Empowerment Advisory Board that advises the AZEC on matters related to program development and administration, Atlanta has not seeded community-based organizations for the purpose of designing and implementing zone programs (HUD, 2000c).

Empowerment zone governance in Chicago has recently undergone a reorganization. However, it remains quite different from Baltimore because of its close association with city government. The original governance structure in Chicago was the Empowerment Zone/Enterprise Community Coordinating Council (Nathan and Wright 1997). The council was composed of thirty-nine members appointed by the mayor under authority provided by the city council. This process was altered and empowerment zone governance is now housed in the city's Office of Budget and Management. In 1999, Chicago organized a network of "Cluster organizations" to provide public outreach, represent the community, and provide technical assistance to zone residents (HUD, 2000d). Although the development of these clusters is intended to provide more community input into the design and operation of zone programs, the cluster organizations do not implement empowerment zone programs.

In Detroit, empowerment zone programs are developed and managed by the Empowerment Zone Development Corporation (EZDC). The EZDC has an executive director and professional staff and includes a board of Directors with representatives of zone neighborhoods and key partners (including city and state government agencies, corporations, and local institutions). Programs are planned and implemented through a committee structure. There are three Neighborhood Review Panels that represent the community of the three regions of the empowerment zone (East, Central, and Southwest) (HUD, 2000e). Unlike Baltimore, members of the community in Detroit represent their interests in zone decision making, but do not actively participate in the implementation of programs.

Zone governance in New York is similar to Baltimore in its distance from city government and tiered structure (Nathan and Wright 1997). The central organization in New York is the New York Empowerment Zone Corporation (NYEZ). NYEZ is comprised of representatives of state and local government, congressional representatives, and representatives of the Manhattan and Bronx regions of the empowerment zone. Two local development corporations are also included in the governance structure; one representing Upper Manhattan and the other representing the South Bronx. These organizations are responsible for developing and implementing zone programs. The Upper Manhattan Empowerment Zone Development Corporation (UMEZ) was created to serve this purpose. The Bronx Overall Economic Development Corporation (BOEDC) existed prior to creation of the empowerment zone. Both these organizations have their own boards and staff (Nathan and Wright 1997). New York is similar to Baltimore in that it has undertaken the creation of a new organization (UMEZ) to develop and implement zone programs. However, in contrast to the Village Centers in Baltimore, UMEZ, and BOEDC are economic development organizations that serve both businesses and zone residents.

The governance situation in Philadelphia/Camden is unique and complex because this empowerment zone was constructed to cross state boundaries. The authorizing legislation for the empowerment zones specified that one of the original six urban empowerment zones must encompass at least two states. Because the zone is in two cities in two states, the governance system is not closely associated with city government and is tiered. A Bi-State Governing Board composed of representatives of four zone communities, government representatives, and representatives of key local institutions is responsible for the empowerment zone. In Philadelphia, three Community Trust Boards (CTBs) have been created. The mayor appoints the chair of each CTB. The CTBs oversee zone programs, in particular the allocation of resources to accomplish the objectives spelled out in the strategic plan (HUD, 2000f). After considerable delay, Camden created the Camden Empowerment Zone Corporation (CEZC); a board of twenty-five voting members directs the corporation including twelve block captains representing zone census tracts, representatives of religious organizations, and zone employers (Nathan and Wright 1997). In March 1998, CEZC hired staff to implement programs. The staff includes four community liaisons (one for each census tract in the zone) that perform outreach services in zone neighborhoods (HUD, 2000g).

Although similarities exist between the governance processes in New York, Philadelphia/Camden, and Baltimore, there are subtle but significant differences in the role that community participation and mobilization play in Baltimore. First, Baltimore has created more organizations to represent smaller, more coherent communities. Second, Village Centers in Baltimore are part of a strategy to develop community capacity and sustain the empowerment zone initiative into the future. While other communities hope to make lasting changes and have taken significant steps to include community representatives in their governance process, Baltimore is trying to spawn community-based institutions that can continue their mission of community service beyond the scope of the empowerment zone initiative. Implicit in Baltimore's approach is the belief that community revitalization is an ongoing problem that must be continually addressed by effective community-based institutions. The ultimate success of Baltimore's strategy to serve zone residents depends upon whether or not the Village Centers survive.

Village Centers as Innovations

Are Baltimore's Village Centers innovative? The Empowerment Zone/Enterprise Community initiative seeks sustainable community revitalization. Baltimore's Village Centers are innovative because the implementation of programs in the empowerment zone is being used as a means of community capacity building. The Village Centers and local community leaders develop capacity by gaining experience operating the Village Centers and implementing large-scale social service programs under the sponsorship of EBMC. Of course, there is a downside to this innovation. The success of programs designed to serve zone residents is contingent on the successful development and operation of the Village Centers. This is much riskier than community participation in planning and decision making; the Village Centers are a key link in the policy implementation process. If that link breaks, zone residents suffer. Additionally, the Village Centers are innovative because they integrate and coordinate the services available to zone residents. Village Center staff help residents to find appropriate services and package them to make zone residents job-ready.

What factors motivated Baltimore's innovative approach to governance? One significant factor is the history and experience Baltimore has using quasi-public nonprofit corporations in development policy. Such institutions are seen locally as an effective means to circumvent cumbersome bureaucratic requirements and to facilitate participation by key stakeholders. Certainly, the quasi-public status of these organizations makes it much easier to include zone businesses in the policy making process. A second factor is the designation of Baltimore as an empowerment zone. It is unlikely that the city would have invested its own resources in the creation of such community-based institutions without empowerment zone designation. Third, the participation of the Rouse Company and its related foundation, the Enterprise Foundation, influenced the decision to create Village Centers. The Village Center is a concept used in several Rouse Company developments. In Columbia, Maryland, a new town developed by the Rouse Company, Village Centers are commercial centers near residential neighborhoods that provide an anchor for the community. Participants in the development of Baltimore's strategic plan noted that Rouse Company representatives suggested the Village Center concept as a means to represent the interests of distinctive communities within the empowerment zone. Finally, EBMC officials viewed the Village Centers as a means to sustain the momentum of community revitalization the empowerment zone programs were designed to stimulate.

What factors limited this innovation? Without question, the greatest limitation that constrained this initiative was community capacity. The problem is that distressed communities tend to lack civic infrastructure, the institutions and leading citizens that stabilize and organize the community to make things happen. EBMC undertook an arduous, costly, and time-consuming task in trying to develop community-based organizations in this context. EBMC solicited applications for the creation of Village Centers and provided technical assistance to those who expressed an interest. The interested parties varied tremendously. In one case, HEBCAC, a preexisting community development organization in East Baltimore applied for recognition as a Village Center. In another case, a lone woman from East Baltimore set out to establish a Village Center. Both applications eventually succeeded.

Once the applications were accepted, the Village Centers were chartered by EBMC and created their own boards. When EBMC was satisfied that administrative processes were sufficiently developed within a Village Center, an administrative agreement between was signed. At that point, Village Centers became eligible for financial support from EBMC and could hire staff and obtain physical space for their operations. However, the ultimate question is whether the Village Centers can survive when EBMC is no longer providing financial and technical support. EBMC officials see this as a problem and as a crucial aspect of their legacy to the city. They have undertaken training and technical assistance to assist the Village Centers in developing survival strategies; in particular, EBMC has encouraged the Village Centers to become community development corporations and to use their influence to gain equity positions in development initiatives in their communities.

The vision of EBMC leaders also constrained the extent to which the Village Centers were innovative by forcing all of them to have similar organizational structures and missions. That was not the vision held by several key participants who contributed to Baltimore's empowerment zone application who contend that the original, innovative vision of the Village Centers was lost. As originally conceived, the Village Centers were not intended to organize according to empowerment zone geography; they were intended to be a vehicle for the advancement of preexisting organizations representing specific communities of interest. For example, a group of business leaders could use an existing community development corporation to band together and organize a Village Center to receive EZ funds to promote their interests in local infrastructure improvements and business service initiatives. Elsewhere, community-based organizations that serve residents could organize as a Village Center to promote their concerns, such as combating crime in open-air drug markets. The point that was lost was that Village Centers would be built upon the strengths of preexisting organizations. This would result in significant variation in the purpose and composition of Village Centers but would contribute to the effectiveness of policy implementation by drawing upon the experience of established organizations (Stoker 1991). When EBMC leaders decided on a plan for eight Village Centers to cover every region of the empowerment zone, Village Centers became more homogenous in form and function. (The revised plan reflects the obvious concern of EBMC officials that all zone residents should be served equally by zone programs.) As a result, each Village Center was assigned to cover a specific geographic region of the zone and to include both businesses and residents as constituents. In addition, EBMC required that Village Centers offer a standard package of services to zone residents. (The Village Centers had some latitude to influence program design by emphasizing selected preapproved components from EBMC's lists.) However, the overall effect of these requirements was to homogenize what otherwise might have been a very rich and varied collection of community-based organizations.

Program Innovations in the Village Centers

Although many similarities exist among the Village Centers, some of them have exhibited a capacity to develop policy innovations. The HEBCAC[2] Village Center has created several complementary programs that integrate job readiness, job placement, and transportation services for zone residents with first-hire agreements with area employers. Under contract with EBMC, HEBCAC operates a workforce development program called "The Gate" that includes social services, job readiness skills, and job training. A reverse-commuting program (supported by a HUD grant and EZ funds) that transports zone residents to suburban locations for jobs complements this program. In addition, HEBCAC has negotiated first-hire agreements with several local employers. HEBCAC staff strives to provide job-ready, transportation-supplied workers to firms in exchange for first-hire commitments. Zone residents who participate are diagnosed and directed to appropriate services to make them job ready, trained, placed, and transported to work.

A second illustration of policy innovation by the Village Centers is the public safety program organized by Washington Village/Pigtown.[3] The program has many components including a public safety advocate who works in the Village Center, block-by-block organization of public safety teams, placement of a community police officer in the Village Center, safe neighborhood design initiatives, placement of probation and parole officers in the Village Center, and federal grant funding for "Weed and Seed" programs in cooperation with the Department of Justice. Perhaps the most innovative aspect of this program is the way in which the public safety program has been integrated into the local court system. The Division of Parole and Probation of the local criminal court has an agreement with the Village Center to direct offenders to perform community service under the direction of Village Center officials. At the Village Center, offenders can meet their probation officer, receive treatment and counseling for substance abuse (if required), and perform community service.

Village Center Conflict in Baltimore

Although they have much in common and often present their concerns to EBMC as a united front, conflict exists among the Village Centers. The primary conflict revolves around the distribution of resources. EBMC distributes resources to support Village Center administration and programs to serve zone residents. However, two problems make this difficult. First, Village Centers represent different numbers of people. The original vision of EBMC officials was that eight Village Centers would be created to serve approximately equal sized populations. However, the decision by HEBCAC to organize itself as a Village Center representing more than one-third of zone residents changed that plan. There are six Village Centers and HEBCAC is by far the largest in terms of population. Second, there is an apparent perception among members of the community that the extent of the "problem" varies from one Village Center to another (and is often inversely related to Village Center size). In other words, many community representatives outside HEBCAC think the problems of urban life are more profound in their neighborhoods. They believe that resource allocations should help reduce this inequity.

These conditions create a recurring pattern for distribution of resources in the EZ governance system. Typically, representatives of HEBCAC argue that EZ monies should be distributed among the Village Centers on the basis of the size of the population each serves. Representatives of other Village Centers argue that money should be divided "equally" among them (meaning the total sum should be divided by six) or that money should be distributed on the basis of the "barriers" that face each local community (these are unspecified, but seem to represent "need" or the "severity of the problem" as indicated above). These two rationales are often joined. To HEBCAC's suggestion for population-based distribution of resources, others respond that the "equal" distribution of money is fairer because it better represents the "barriers" that communities face in implementing EZ initiatives.

The ongoing disagreement about distribution of funds delayed the development of the Village Centers. In order to receive a budget and hire staff, the Village Centers were required to sign "administrative agreements" with EBMC. The agreements were delayed while representatives of the Village Centers disputed the basis for distributing funds for administrative expenses. EBMC allowed the Village Centers to work out their differences and in the end, a compromise was struck that provided a larger allocation to HEBCAC, but not so much as would have been provided by a population-based distribution. That was not the end of the dispute however. It is common for the Village Centers to bargain about resource allocation as programs are developed and funded. Disputes over the distribution of funds from EBMC have been a source of frustration. One EBMC official suggested that the disputes indicate that the Village Centers place too much emphasis on funding from EBMC and too little emphasis on using EZ funds to leverage other resources from other sources in the community.

Delays in Establishing the Village Centers
Delay was a significant factor in the process of establishing the Village Centers that resulted in delays in the implementation of programs to benefit zone residents. The first delay resulted from the process required to create the Village Centers. This was a complicated process because EBMC officials established extensive guidelines about how Village Centers were to be composed. It was necessary for each Village Center to organize a board that represented the various stakeholders in each area of the zone. The effect of this requirement was to place the resolution of community conflict at the doorstep of the Village Centers. Although EBMC did provide technical assistance to mediate conflicts, several Village Centers were years in development as a result of community conflict. The creation of the Village Centers was further complicated by extensive administrative and financial management requirements imposed by EBMC. EBMC has a culture of accountability that it imposed upon the Village Centers. While this has doubtless value as a source of integrity in public management, it strained community capacity and delayed development of the Village Centers.

The second delay was for planning at the Village Centers. Village Centers have extensive planning responsibilities (including land use plans, public safety plans, family support strategies, and job readiness plans). EBMC officials wanted the Village Centers to be serious participants in the design of service options for zone residents. This was intended to give the Village Centers a stake in program development and to allow them to tune EBMC's broad initiatives to reflect the distinctive characteristics or needs of their communities. However, the effect of this requirement was that services to zone residents were delayed as the Village Centers undertook extensive planning processes. These plans were also a potential source of community conflict but more significantly, challenged community activists to develop coherent service proposals that met the rigorous standards imposed by EBMC. The lengthy proposals explain budget requests, service options, and service coordination. In essence, the Village Centers were held responsible for bringing coherence to the fragmented array of social services available to zone residents in Baltimore.

Once plans were approved, services to zone residents were delayed while each of the Village Centers geared up to offer services. Some delays were encountered because Village Centers had difficulty finding appropriate space. Others had extensive searches for staff or frequent turnover. Programs had to be marketed in local communities. Village Centers were also directed to establish their own contracting relationships with vendors that had been pre approved by EBMC. However, negotiating with contractors was time consuming.

The delays noted above were experienced by Village Centers that succeeded in meeting EBMC's expectations and requirements. Not all did. Harlem Park and Poppleton Village Centers were slow to complete their administrative agreements and so were operated for extended periods by volunteers. Two Village Centers have had serious, ongoing problems implementing programs to serve their residents. In Harlem Park and Self-Motivated Community People, the job readiness and training programs offered to zone residents are managed by Goodwill Industries. The Village Centers entered this partnership, a forced marriage engineered by EBMC, when they were unable to manage the programs on their own. In addition, the Self-Motivated Community People's Village Center has experienced several leadership and administrative problems over the years. Recently, financial support for the Village Center was suspended.

Who Is Empowered?
Empower Baltimore Management Corporation is a quasi-public entity with a board dominated by the city's elite. Although many of their decisions have been controversial, officials at Empower Baltimore are only indirectly accountable to the public. Shortly after Baltimore was designated as an empowerment zone, the board used its power to establish priorities because the list of programs contained in the application was deemed too ambitious and some members doubted the emphasis placed upon social services. Matthew DeVito, founding chairman of the EBMC board said: "We can't choose too many things. The board is putting a circle around the big things that matter" (Segal 1995a). Other members of the board expressed skepticism about spending on social programs. Bernard Siegel, a founding member of the EBMC board, indicated that he rated many of the social programs in the application as low priority because he felt that spending EZ money that way would have little effect: "The most we could spend would be a drop in the bucket compared to what's being spent now" (Segal 1995b). Empower Baltimore empowered the city's elite.

The board made other key decisions that influenced the distribution of benefits in the zone. Business was seen as a special clientele that required professional services and financial assistance. This resulted in the creation of the two-track implementation process that insulated business clients from the community conflict that constrained development of the Village Centers and delivery of services to zone residents. Although Baltimore's application for empowerment zone designation included business finance initiatives, including a One-Stop-Capital-Shop and a high-risk loan fund, the application proposed to finance these programs through leveraging. However, subsequently the board decided to use empowerment zone social service block grant funding to finance business loan programs. Business clients were empowered by Empower Baltimore.

What about zone residents? With the exception of HEBCAC, the Village Centers are creatures of Empower Baltimore. Do the Village Centers represent genuine empowerment of the local community or the realization of an organizational plan imposed by Empower Baltimore? Officials at Empower Baltimore have been paternalistic toward the Village Centers, creating demanding requirements and rigorous oversight procedure. They have used their power of the purse to discipline Village Centers that do not satisfy their expectations. However, the problem confronting EBMC officials was vexing: How to empower residents in communities that lack social capital? If Empower Baltimore officials had not created Village Centers, large segments of the community would have never mobilized. If the community had mobilized at all, many parts of it would have failed to establish the foundation required to make a lasting contribution to policy making in the zone. Empower Baltimore seeded and nurtured these organizations; whether they survive and grow can only be known with time. If the Village Centers do survive, Empower Baltimore will have created a genuine, lasting source of empowerment.

Bibliography

Segal, Eric. 1995a. "Job Training Takes Priority in Empowerment Zone: Board Votes to Put Social Programs on Back Burner." *Baltimore Sun*, 6 October, 1A.

Segal, Eric. 1995b. "Changes Anger Zone Residents: Empowerment Board Acted Without Enough Input, Critics Contend." *Baltimore Sun*, October 16, 1B.

HUD, 2000a. "Introduction to the RC/EZ/EC initiative." Report available on the Department of Housing and Urban Development website. http://www.hud.gov/offices/cpd/ezec/about/ezecinit.cfm

HUD, 2000b. "Key Principles." Report available on the Department of Housing and Urban Development website. http://www.hud.gov/offices/cpd/ezec/about/keyprincipals.cfm

HUD, 2000c. "Atlanta, PERMS Report 2000." Report available on the Department of Housing and Urban Development website.
http://www5.hud.gov/urban/perms/perms.asp
HUD, 2000d. "Chicago, PERMS Report 2000." Report available on the Department of Housing and Urban Development website.
http://www5.hud.gov/urban/perms/perms.asp
HUD, 2000e. "Detroit, PERMS Report 2000." Report available on the Department of Housing and Urban Development website.
http://www5.hud.gov/urban/perms/perms.asp
HUD, 2000f. "Philadelphia, PERMS Report 2000." Report available on the Department of Housing and Urban Development website.
http://www5.hud.gov/urban/perms/perms.asp
HUD, 2000g. "Camden, PERMS Report 2000." Report available on the Department of Housing and Urban Development website.
http://www5.hud.gov/urban/perms/perms.asp
Nathan, Richard, and David Wright. 1997. *Building a Community Plan for Strategic Change: Findings from the First Round Assessment of the Empowerment Zone/Enterprise Community Initiative.* Albany, N. Y.: The Nelson A. Rockefeller Institute of Government, State University of New York.
Stoker, Robert. 1987. "Baltimore: The Self-Evaluating City?" In *The Politics of Urban Development,* Clarence Stone and Heywood Sanders, ed. Lawrence, Kansas: University of Kansas Press.
Stoker, Robert. 1991. *Reluctant Partners: Implementing Federal Policy.* Pittsburgh, Penn.: University of Pittsburgh Press.
Stone, Clarence, 1987. "The Study of the Politics of Urban Development" In *The Politics of Urban Development,* Clarence Stone and Heywood Sanders, ed. Lawrence, Kansas: University of Kansas Press.
Stone, Clarence N.. 1989. *Regime Politics: Governing Atlanta 1946-1988.* Lawrence, Kansas: University of Kansas Press.

Endnotes

NOTE: The author would like to thank the staff of Minnesota's Office of the Legislative Auditor for the opportunity to work on the report that motivated this research and for access to their data.

[1] The author was associated with two HUD sponsored evaluations of Baltimore's empowerment zone and completed extensive field research including analysis of government documents, review of EBMC documents and reports, review of Village Center documents, personal interviews with key participants, and participant observation of meetings of EBMC, its committees, and the Advisory Council. The case analysis presented here is based upon this research.

[2] HEBCAC is a community-based organization in East Baltimore located near the Johns Hopkins Hospital and medical campus. The organization has an active partnership with Hopkins and enjoys financial support from the hospital. HEBCAC existed prior to the empowerment zone initiative, but now also is sponsored by EBMC as a Village Center.

[3] The awkward name of this Village Center reflects tension over a neighborhood in transition. Pigtown is the historic name of a working class neighborhood located in Southwest Baltimore near the sports stadiums (Camden Yards and M&T Bank Stadium) and industrial properties Those who hope to market the community to attract new residents and investment refer to it as Washington Village.

Chapter 6

Marilyn Klotz

Local Government and Community Social Service Providers as the Social Safety Net in Six Case Studies in a Midwestern State

Introduction
This chapter examines public-private collaboration at the local level in the area of poverty alleviation.[1] This Midwestern state has a unique system of locally elected government officials, known as township trustees, who provide general assistance to the poor in their communities. These public servants, in conjunction with community social service providers, form the safety net of last resort for low-income residents of the state. In light of recent welfare reform changes enacted in the past six years, a study was undertaken to examine the impact of social policy changes on township trustees and community agencies serving the poor. The increased reliance on the private sector to produce services previously administered by the federal and state governments has been dubbed by some political scientists devolution through the nonprofit sector (Nathan 1996). Some providers and trustees have noticed an increased number of people requesting township assistance since welfare reform. At the same

time, there is the potential for new partnerships between trustees and local community agencies. These partnerships can target services to the unique community needs and recipient characteristics of the area. Such a social safety net has the potential to target services to specific needs of recipients and to provide personalized casework.

A brief history of welfare reform in the state will assist in better understanding the changes that have taken place over the past six years and their impact on local poverty relief efforts (Pirog 2000). Like many other states, this state shifted from a welfare program with an education and training focus to one with a strong "Work First" orientation in the mid-1990's. The rationale behind this change was a belief that employment and job experience of any type would better position welfare recipients to improve their employment skills and eventually become economically independent. The state has a two-year limit on continuous public assistance receipt and a five-year lifetime limit. In addition, the state may impose a sanction consisting of denial of the adult portion of the welfare grant if recipients fail to abide by welfare reform requirements. Welfare recipients rely on township trustees and community social service providers to supplement cash assistance payments or to provide assistance when the family is sanctioned or has reached the time limit.

Unlike other states with a state-administered General Assistance Program, this state has a unique system of local township trustees who serve as the last public resource for poor families (Byers et al. 2000). The state's 92 counties are divided into 1008 townships, for an average of about 11 townships per county. Township government and the procedure for laying out township boundaries were established in 1790 in the Acts of the Northwest Territories, before the state was admitted to the Union. The number of townships varies from county to county, from as few as four to as many as twenty-one.

Originally called the "overseer of the poor," a term that first appeared in the Elizabethan Poor Laws of 1572, the township trustee has primary responsibility for the provision of emergency poor relief for residents of the township. Some townships operate fire departments, both professionally paid and volunteer. Some townships are also responsible for maintaining township parks and cemeteries and cutting weeds along roads. A few townships operate homeless shelters and food pantries. Some with even more comprehensive services provide a variety of other personal social services including budgeting, job search, and other work orientation programs. In townships with a population of less than 8000, the trustee also serves as township assessor, whose major duty is to establish the value of real and personal property of residents for tax purposes. As a result, trustee duties and the amount of time available for poor relief vary considerably across townships.

The residents of each township elect the trustee to a four-year term. A three-person elected township board is responsible for adopting the annual township budget, imposing tax levies, and setting policy for the distribution of poor relief within the guidelines provided by state law. Though some townships receive funds from other sources, the majority of poor relief funds come from local property taxes. The law requires uniform budgeting of poor relief funds and the filing of such budgets with the county auditor, who then reimburses the vendors for vouchers supplied to poor relief recipients. For poor relief, the state mandates the use of a standardized application form, standardized financial reporting to the State Board of Accounts for all township income and expenditures on an annual basis, and notification procedures within seventy-two hours of application and other such procedural guidelines. In providing poor relief, the trustees may require work in exchange for poor relief benefits, may provide work training and other rehabilitation programs to assist recipients, and may ask relatives of applicants to assist with material relief. Trustees are to cooperate with local community agencies also providing assistance to low-income residents. State standards for poor relief mandate that townships must have criteria for determining eligibility, although these criteria vary based on local community standards.

While there are state standards to be met, township trustees, in comparison to other public assistance programs, have considerable discretion in the use of the funds they disperse for poor relief. There is no entitlement for poor relief assistance from the trustee. Local residents apply for assistance by completing a standardized state form requesting assistance for such short-term needs as rent payments, food, utilities, and medical bills. The trustee, following state guidelines and the eligibility criteria set by his or her township board, then determines if the applicant will receive the assistance requested.

Traditionally, township trustees have provided emergency services while initiating a plan with clients to move toward self-sufficiency. Such plans have included interim referrals to state and federal support programs for which the family qualifies such as Food Stamps, Supplemental Security Income (SSI), energy assistance, and the old Aid to Families with Dependent Children (AFDC) program. In addition, trustees make referrals to other community agencies providing specific services to address needs such as child care, employment and training services, emergency food assistance, and alcohol and drug rehabilitation.

The trustees refer applicants to a variety of community agencies (primarily private not-for-profit and public agencies) for ongoing assistance with their basic needs, including Food Stamps for food assistance, the local Energy Assistance Program for utilities, and Temporary Assistance for Needy Families (TANF) and SSI for income support. They make referrals to local churches and other religious organizations for emergency assistance with food and clothing. At this time, they make few referrals to agencies providing job training, education, or employment services, though some of those interviewed indicated increases in their referrals in these areas. Though trustees regularly refer to local community agencies, few of those agencies identify the trustees as a primary referral agency they use. A study of community social service providers found that trustees were less likely to be a part of their referral networks. In general, social service providers that were interviewed for the study report limited contact with township trustees. It is clear that in many communities, the trustees are not well connected to the local referral networks.

This chapter draws on data from two main sources. First, data on the township trustees consist of a mail survey of township trustees conducted in 1999 and thirty-six personal interviews with trustees in six case study sites (Byers et al. 2000). While the mail survey is a representative sample of the trustee population, the trustee interviews are not necessarily representative of the views of all trustees. Second, data on community social service providers comes from personal interviews with 295 executive directors of agencies in the six case study sites (Reingold et al. 2000). The case studies consist of two urban, two mixed, and two rural study sites. These research findings are exploratory and are not intended to present findings that could be generalized beyond those organizations included in the study. The final data set is not a random sample and the findings should be considered in that context. A detailed description of the data collection methods can be found at the end of this chapter.

The State's Economic Context

As true for the nation at large, at the same time that this state undertook welfare reform, the economy in the region was booming. By 1998, the statewide unemployment rate was 3.1 percent (Reingold, et al. 2000), compared to 4.9 percent in 1994. The three-year poverty average declined from 11.8 percent (1993-1995) to 8.6 percent (1996-1998). Not surprisingly, with such a strong economy, the number of people receiving cash assistance declined considerably over this period of time. The public assistance caseload in the state peaked in January 1994 at 71,141 households. In 1995, the caseload declined moderately to 67,123 households as welfare reform was initiated. Since that year, the further decline in caseloads has been precipitous, reaching 36,961 households in January 1998. The TANF rolls have continued to decline to 29,330 households, but in 2000 they showed some signs of leveling off. As a result, since 1994, there has been an almost 60 percent decline in the welfare caseload.

All of the counties selected for case studies have experienced substantial declines in TANF participation since 1994, with the highest rate of decline in rural areas. While one urban case study county continues to have the highest rate of welfare participation in the state, the other urban case study county has an unusually low rate of welfare participation for an urban area. All together, the case study communities contained 51 percent of the state's 1999 welfare caseload, compared to 47 percent in 1995.

Overview of Changes

Despite the fact that on average, the agencies interviewed are expanding operations, adding thirteen new staff members and experiencing budget increases of 33 percent from 1994 to 1998, about three-quarters of the social service agencies reported not being able to meet the demand for services since the state's welfare reforms began in 1995 (Reingold et al. 2000). There have been substantial increases in the demand for services, with secular not-for-profit providers reporting the largest increases in service demand and government agencies the least likely to report an increase. For-profit social service organizations have experienced the most substantial growth in staffing levels. For most of the sample, 80 percent of staff in an agency have a college education or less. In fact, most respondents' agencies are staffed by people without a master's degree. The exception is faith-based organizations, many of which are directed by ministers with graduate degrees in religion.

Most agencies have experienced budget increases since the beginning of welfare reform, with the largest budget increases occurring among for-profit organizations. Another trend over the study period is an increased reliance on federal funds. There has been a substantial shift toward federal resources since welfare reform, while state and local funds have remained the same or declined as a percentage of the budget. For-profit organizations in particular have increased their reliance on federal money while governmental providers have actually seen a decline in the portion of their budget from federal funds. At the same time, providers complain that there are too many different funding streams for federal money and that the eligibility criteria are too complex (Reingold et al. 2000).

Social service providers in the study report very high rates of interagency cooperation and collaboration (Reingold et al. 2000). Almost four-fifths of agencies (79.7 percent) report active service or program coordination with a not-for-profit organization. Almost three-quarters (74.8 percent) report active service or program coordination with a government agency. Over one-third (35.9 percent) report active service or program coordination with a for-profit firm. Almost 60 percent of nonprofit, nonreligious organizations have joined a service network. The two urban counties appear to have organizations that are more likely to have joined a social service network since welfare reform. While a majority (69.6 percent) of agency ties existed prior to welfare reform, a substantial number are new. Overall, approximately one-third of all agency-level organizational ties have developed since welfare reform. This finding appears to indicate that welfare reform is having a profound impact on the development of new professional ties among social service providers. Another finding is that agencies with increasing, as well as agencies with decreasing, levels of demand for services have established more new relationships, while agencies reporting no change in demand for services have developed fewer new ties.

Welfare reform has also heightened the sense of interagency competition, particularly among organizations serving people in the two urban county case studies (Reingold, et al. 2000). According to some respondents, the welfare department has been sending mixed messages, encouraging interagency collaboration at the same time as developing competitive contracts that pit one agency against another. One respondent described the current social service business environment as "coopitition" underscoring his opinion that agencies are being asked to pursue conflicting goals (Reingold et al. 2000). The difficulty in determining competitors and cooperators has led to a system where informal partnerships (or cartels) develop among social service providers. Cooperation is likely when the agency's executive director has a personal relationship with another organization that fosters trust and certainty. However, when the executive director leaves the organization and that personal relationship is gone, it may be replaced with more suspicious and competitive interactions. Social service providers have responded to the competing pressures to collaborate and compete by developing "flexible specialization." Agencies are increasingly organizing the production of services into specialized areas that are flexible enough to withstand sudden changes in administrative rules and funding streams. The result of these adaptations is the development of new programs and initiatives that are locally designed and implemented with no real continuity across geographic locations. This finding underscores the need for administrative changes that attempt to design services for the particular needs of specific clients.

Few of the trustees are active participants in the local mechanisms in their counties for planning and coordination of social services. In some counties, these mechanisms may not be well developed. In some counties, the trustees may not be viewed as potential resources or service providers and so may not be included in these local coordinating organizations. In other counties, particular trustees may not see their involvement in these mechanisms as useful, given the low numbers of poor relief applicants they serve on an annual basis. In some counties, trustees do have organized regular meetings to share information and engage in problem solving. These local trustee mechanisms may provide opportunities to link the trustees as a group to other local planning efforts.

While the results of the mail survey suggest that trustees make use of the community social service network within their communities by referring applicants and recipients to other providers, the opposite is not necessarily the case. In the interviews conducted with executive directors of community social service agencies in the six case studies in seven research counties, only 25 percent of respondents mentioned the township trustee's office as a resource for their applicants. Likewise, in the client survey, many current and former welfare recipients were not aware of the services offered by the township trustees. As low-income individuals reach their time limits or if the economy should falter, the township trustees will play an integral social safety net role.

A phone survey of current and former welfare recipients found that not all potential clients may be aware of the assistance available from the township trustees (Pirog 2000). In asking respondents where they seek help, the township trustee was listed as one of the options that could be selected for a variety of kinds of assistance. Shortly into the phone interviewing process, an explanation about the trustees had to be added to the interview protocol because so many respondents did not know who the township trustee was and what kind of assistance was available through the trustee's office. Results of the client survey indicate that the trustees provide more help to welfare recipients in some areas of need than in others. Over all, for welfare clients, family and friends provide the majority of help that they receive meeting basic needs, regardless of the need category. The township trustees provided the most assistance in addressing housing and utility needs for recipients. With regard to helping with a place to stay, the trustees, religious organizations, and community organizations were close in their frequency of providing help to welfare recipients, with about 15 percent for the trustees. Our research indicates that trustees are the most frequent source of help with rental assistance after family and friends, but still helping fewer than 30 percent of welfare recipients. More than a third of the welfare recipients contacted from the phone interview reported receiving help with utilities from the township trustees, more than any other agency type. For food assistance, less than 20 percent of the clients reported getting assistance from the trustees, well behind the level of help received from religious and community organizations. These areas of assistance (food, rent, utilities) are the ones for which the township trustees have traditionally had major responsibility. Though fewer welfare recipients received clothing assistance from township trustees than other organizations, trustees still helped 20 percent of recipients who received clothing assistance. Less than 10 percent of welfare recipients received help from the trustees to purchase diapers or toys for children. Very few welfare recipients received help from the trustees for child care (4 percent), transportation (2 percent), or emotional support (2 percent); results that are not surprising given that community agencies are better equipped to offer these services than the trustees.

Besides providing assistance directly themselves, township trustees also make referrals for assistance to other agencies in their local communities. A substantial majority of trustees (78 percent) interviewed reported that the quality of social services in their township was good or very good (Byers, et al. 2000). The same percentage, although not necessarily the same trustees, reported that services were accessible or very accessible to people in need in their community. The trustees who judged services less accessible tended to be from more rural townships.

In the mail survey of township trustees, respondents were asked to list up to six different agencies to which they made referrals (Byers, et al. 2000). Of the 503 trustees who completed the mail survey, 396 respondents (79 percent) listed at least one agency. Of those listed agencies for which trustees indicated an organizational type (1225 agencies total), 408 were non-profit religious, 436 were nonprofit nonreligious, 348 were public (government) agencies, and only 33 were for-profit. In the religious nonprofit category, local churches and ministerial associations account for 160 of the 408 referrals. Trustees referred applicants to the Salvation Army 101 times, and to St. Vincent de Paul (a Catholic charitable society) 30 times. The nonprofit, nonreligious category (436 referrals) includes a substantial number of referrals to Community Action Program (CAP) agencies, and affiliated programs, such as the Energy Assistance Program (EAP). Two hundred twenty-one trustees listed a CAP or affiliated agency as part of their referral network. In responding to the needs of the elderly, 30 trustees listed area agencies on aging. Other referrals included the American Red Cross (24), the United Way (9), and to local service organizations such as the Lion's Club (5), Jaycees (1) and the American Legion (1). Among public (government) organizations receiving referrals from trustees, the majority were state agencies providing services traditionally thought of as "welfare," such as TANF, WIC, Food Stamps, and Medicaid. Of the 348 public agencies in trustee referral networks, 215 fell into the welfare category. Other public agency referrals were to housing programs, Workforce Development and Social Security. For-profit organizations comprised only a very small part of trustees' referral networks. Nine trustees reported referring applicants to utility companies for assistance with bills, other referrals included temporary employment agencies, medical or dental care providers, a local grocery store, a child care center, a bank, and a funeral director.

Evidence from the mail survey indicates that trustees are giving relatively less emphasis to job training and placement programs in their referral patterns, compared to programs offering mainly emergency services (Byers et al. 2000). The mail survey question on services provided by referral organizations garnered 1527 distinct responses (this number is somewhat higher than the total number of referral organizations because some trustees mentioned multiple services for a single organization). Of the 1527 different services listed, job training and placement programs received only 63 mentions (4.1 percent of the total). The only other services provided by referral agencies which might assist with job placement are clothing, with 98 mentions (6.4 percent), child care, with 20 mentions (1.3 percent) and transportation, with 13 mentions (.9 percent).

By contrast, emergency services comprised the vast majority of service types (Byers 2000). Food assistance was the largest category, with 403 mentions (26.4 percent). Utility assistance was second, with 327 mentions (21.4 percent). Housing assistance (which includes emergency shelter for the homeless and rental assistance) was third, with 193 mentions (12.6 percent). The fourth largest category was general cash assistance, with 127 mentions (8.3 percent). The fifth largest category was assistance with medical bills, with 102 mentions (6.7 percent). Together, these five forms of short-term, emergency help account for 75.4 percent of all referral services mentioned by the trustees.

These data on referrals are consistent with the general perception that the proper role of the trustees in assisting the poor is primarily to provide emergency services. This view is long-standing and is held by both the public in general and by a majority of the trustees themselves. In the interviews, trustees noted more changes in their referral patterns since 1994 than in other areas of service delivery. Over one-third (13 of 36) of the trustees reported changes in their referral patterns since 1994, and most of those changed were geared toward assuring employment opportunities for recipients. Four trustees made more referrals to job training programs, and three made more referrals to job location services. Referrals to educational programs and services saw increases by three trustees. One trustee reported additional referrals for a food bank, and three increased their referrals for utility assistance. The increases in referrals to employment related programs suggest that some trustees may be trying to address more the root of recipients' lack of income rather than continuing to simply provide emergency assistance, thus expanding the focus of trustees' work.

With increased experience in office, several trustees in the interviews indicated they were becoming more effective in making referrals. "I've learned that there's no sense in referring somebody some place if you absolutely know that they are not going to get any assistance there. So I try to refer them to the places that I think will help them (Byers 2000)."

A number of the trustees send applicants with a written referral to other agencies in order to verify that they have interviewed the person. Food pantries and other such agencies then may look more favorably on the request if the agency knows that the applicant has been sent by the trustee.

Few of the trustees had formal follow-up systems in place for verifying that applicants received the services from other agencies to which they were referred. One trustee said, "some agencies send out a referral form that they send back to us. . . .Other times it's a phone call." Most felt they found out informally by talking to the other service providers or by talking to the recipients themselves when they returned to the office for additional services. In small communities, the trustees said they knew if people were doing better "because a lot of them I know personally. You know if they are doing alright now."

Local communities have both formal and informal mechanisms designed to foster collaboration and coordination among local service providers (Reingold et al. 2000). Some of these mechanisms are mandated by state agencies for planning purposes or for the disbursement of state funds to local providers. For those mechanisms that are mandated, some counties and regions have very active and involved intermediary agencies while others are less well developed and organized. Such local coordinating mechanisms focused on services to low-income families and individuals include the Step Ahead Councils, the Local Planning Councils, and other local welfare-to-work programs. Step Ahead is a comprehensive, statewide process designed to coordinate a variety of services to individuals, children, and families in their communities. Local Step Ahead Councils in communities help channel resources to fund local programs for child care and other services. The Local Planning Councils, mandated under Indiana's state plan for TANF, have included representatives from key public and private agencies to develop action plans designed to help move welfare recipients toward self-sufficiency. In addition, some communities have developed other broad local planning and coordinating groups to assist them in delivering a variety of social services in an effective and efficient manner.

In the site visit interviews, trustees were asked about their involvement in some of these local mechanisms (Byers et al. 2000). Few of the trustees interviewed reported regular involvement in these efforts. Less than 20 percent (7 out of 36) of the trustees were involved in either Step Ahead or local welfare-to-work programs. Only six trustees were involved in the Local Planning Councils. And some of those trustees were also involved in Step Ahead. It is clear that among those interviewed, involvement in these local efforts was not extensive. Several explanations for this low level of involvement could be advanced. In some of the local communities, these local mechanisms are not well developed and well organized themselves. They may not actively reach out to trustees and others who may not be seen as part of the traditional social service network. In other communities, these mechanisms, because some of them are responsible for the distribution of funds, may have become powerful and influential. They could be somewhat exclusive about what other agencies are invited to be a part of the process. For some townships, the trustees who distribute little poor relief may see little benefit for their involvement in such efforts. In fact, some of the trustees in rural communities providing little poor relief had not heard of some of these organizations and their work. It could be that in some communities these local mechanisms go by other names, thereby making it difficult to assess trustee knowledge about these local planning and coordinating resources.

For some township trustees interviewed, it was clear that they saw their involvement in these coordinating organizations as helpful to their work in providing poor relief. They reported attending meetings themselves or sending staff to represent the township office. For them, these coordinating meetings were an opportunity to network with other service providers in the community to discuss and resolve common problems and issues impacting local social service providers. One trustee said, "I found out about this new service that I can refer people to for help with their utilities and another one that has opened for domestic violence (Byers et al. 2000)."

Several counties where interviews were conducted had regular (sometimes monthly) meetings of all trustees in the county to exchange information and plan coordinated county efforts. In some cases, the poor-relief supervisors had additional meetings. Sometimes, community organizations are invited to these meetings to discuss the services they provide, thus informing the trustees about available county resources. In some cases, these meetings may also include the major utility companies to find out the kind of assistance they are offering for people having difficulty paying their bills.

Only a few trustees provide services beyond those that meet emergency basic needs. Most trustees have not changed their services or the way in which they provide those services in response to welfare reforms in the state.

The Urban Sites
The following quotations[2] from interviews with township trustees offer an idea of trustees' views of their role in the community and their commitment to community service in their townships.[3]

I think there is always going to be a need for us because we fill a void. Because there is no other agency that can help on an ongoing basis.

Sometimes, I get, maybe, a little too personally involved in it. But, I try to motivate them. I try to explain to them that, if you're standing down here in the ground and you want to get on top of the building, how are you going to get there? You can't jump from here to there. You have to put a ladder up and go one step at a time.

I had one situation happen here, it was about five years ago maybe more than that. What happened was we had a man in a van that was staying over at the Food Stamp office. On their property. He used that as his address. Well, he called our office here and the girls were telling him, 'well sir, you are really a transient. You have to have a legal address.' He says, 'Well, I'm living over here and they told me to give their address.' And the girls said, 'well, I'm sorry sir. Unless you have a legal residence, we can't help you.'

So what I normally do is a give one-way bus ticket back home. Yeah, back where they came from.

The two counties included in this study are two of the most urban counties in the state as measured by density of population per square mile. Typical of urban communities nationwide, these counties have larger minority populations, slightly higher poverty rates, and lower home-ownership rates compared to the state average. One county contains 15 percent of the state population. Higher poverty (and urban) counties generally have larger agencies as measured by staff size. Yet, the county poverty rate is inversely related to the rate of change in staff growth since welfare reform began.

Providers in one of the urban county case studies saw the portion of their budgets constituted by federal funds cut almost in half, declining from 44.6 percent of the overall operating budgets in 1994 to 26.7 percent in 1998.

In at least one urban county, while the county contains one of the largest cities in the state, the county itself is a unique blend of urban, suburban and rural communities, each of which developed independently of the others. From 1940 to 1970, the county gained a quarter million people attracted to jobs in heavy industry. However, since 1970, the county has experienced considerable population decline that has only recently begun to turn around. The jobless rate is lower than might be anticipated, representing both some increase in available jobs and the county's decline in population, so that it is not clear that economic conditions have improved as much as the low unemployment rate might indicate. Because of considerable strife among metropolitan areas at the turn of the last century, less than perfect trust and cooperation exist today among the communities in the county. Each individual community in the county and each ethnic neighborhood and population has developed independently from each other. There is a tradition, therefore, of independent action in the face of a crisis or problem. This may account for the fact that there are more than 2,000 social service-related agencies in the county. Because each community has developed separate networks of organizations, and because even the existing intermediary organizations have been unable to suppress competition, there are many cases of overlapping services located short distances from each other.

Because it is composed of members of many interested groups, including business, academic, nonprofit organizations and government

agencies, the Welfare to Work Council has been able to broaden awareness of the changing welfare environment. The Council has brought
groups together to work on a one-stop data collection and retrieval system and initiated a study of agencies' data systems and system requirements. Yet, problems remain. One trustee laments that "we never get
information on any newly available services. I've got to call around. I
might hear about it from a recipient (unpublished transcript of interview
with township trustee)." At the same time, a trustee remarks "there is a
lot of duplication. Things like housing with all this funding that went out
this year to all these different agencies to study the problem of homeless-
ness."

Respondents from the organizations surveyed did not indicated that
much change had occurred in the services they provide since welfare reform began, nor did they indicate that they plan much change in their
service agendas in the near future. "We always offer food pantry. We
encourage them to take something from the food pantry. We help them
with utilities, except for phone. We do not have any facilities to house
perishables here, so we write vouchers for the grocery stores to supplement what we do have. We have helped with rent in some cases and prescriptions (unpublished transcript of interview with township trustee)."
There were also indications in the interviews that social service providers
are beginning to see the value to their clients of stronger regional cooperation, especially in the areas of "growing" jobs through regional economic development efforts and in the development of regional public
transportation systems. "The biggest one we use, probably, is Southwest
Mobile Service Center. Mary has been over there for years, and knows
me well and knows my sister well, who is my secretary. And, you know,
we discuss cases, when we can help and when we can't. A lot of times
she will have information I don't have. And I'll have information that
she doesn't." One agency reported success in placing clients through
neighborhood networks based on common ethnic heritage.

Many organizations reported significant projects being conducted with
other organizations, for example, training prospective employees to meet
the requirements of specific employers. A number of joint projects involved children's health and family and youth activities. Many projects
were related to economic development, transportation, and support for
entrepreneurship in the region. Others involved purchasing housing stock
for rehabilitation and providing shelter, food, and health care for women,
minorities, and those infected with the HIV virus. Respondents reported
that they felt increasing pressure to collaborate, both from the obvious

economic reasons, and from a desire to fulfill their organizational missions.

The most significant consequence of welfare reform for providers in the county may be the need to overcome their reluctance to work together to achieve economies of scale and preserve resources to better serve the whole county's population. The Welfare to Work Council has encouraged collaboration by sponsoring a study of computer compatibility among providers, and by bringing elements together for information sharing and planning. The county's response to poverty could be better coordinated, and this might serve to reduce the stress and confusion of recipients. A successful response to welfare reform demands a willingness to give up turf—to collaborate and cooperate with other organizations. In addition, innovative funding mechanisms help organizations thrive in the uncertain climate of welfare reform grants and contracts. Other variables key to successful adaptation include having a more holistic approach to addressing poverty, rather than focusing on specific services or client populations; and a willingness to form or join networks.

In one case study county, many CSS respondents acknowledged that eligibility determination had become more formalized since 1995, and that verification of need and eligibility is now more common than in the past.

The other urban county has seen an economic boom over the past decade. Because there are so many places that need more employees, it has been relatively easy for welfare recipients to get jobs. While major manufacturing plants have closed, two of the closed plants now house employment service programs. There are two specific small business initiatives that target low-income neighborhoods. Because of the strength of the current economy, several employment organizations report that employers want help obtaining employees. Thus, employers enter into contracts with agencies for assistance in recruiting, screening, and providing training for prospective employees. Furthermore, a public economic development corporation has partnered with a university to create a database of employers' needs that will be accessible in schools and libraries throughout the region. This database is intended to expedite the process of matching job seekers with employers.

A good example of the magnitude of organizational change is shown by one religious-based organization. Ten years ago the organization served only disabled people, but now that is only a third of their clientele. This organization has developed many programs to assist welfare recipients move into the workforce. Another group of service providers that have become significantly involved in providing employment services along with their traditional services in the areas of recreation, senior adult activities, child care, basic education, and emergency assistance are the various community centers. Thirteen neighborhood centers are located in low-income neighborhoods and many of them have added welfare to work contracts and employment specialists to their organizational structure.

Public-private partnerships have also prospered under welfare reform. In 1997, the coordination of day care and the determination of eligibility for day care subsidies was transferred from the county government to a private provider organization. Another organization has partnered with schools and public housing facilities to offer neighborhood programs for children and youth. One director said that her center obtained a welfare-to-work contract in 1999 to train forklift operators who are "hard to employ" welfare recipients. After a week of job readiness training, clients are placed in a forklift operator's position with the agency's for-profit partner. Welfare-to-work participants in this program are eligible for child care subsidies and can receive additional assistance up to a total cost of $1000 for employment barriers, such as rent or utility deposits, fees for a driver's license, unpaid traffic fines, and so forth.

Another example of collaboration is a community center that partnered with a religious-based organization to establish a career service program in 1995. Through this program, participants prepare to earn their GED and obtain job training plus the needed supportive assistance for things such as housing, utilities, and food. The director of such a center regards this type of partnership as typical of the collaboration fostered by welfare reform. He reported that he "sees more true collaboration among service providers, such as his Center's work" with other providers (Reingold et. al 2000). He believes that agencies are "moving beyond parallel service delivery to integration of services." An educational institute involves collaboration among for-profit, nonprofit, and religious organizations with substantial funding from a private endowment that is administered by the city. Agencies have contracted with this organization to recruit and train people from seven inner-city neighborhoods for positions in downtown hotels and restaurants. This institute conducts it's training at a church. Not only does this church provide the space for the institute's training, they also assist trainees with other needs, such as housing. This church is renovating space for a transitional housing program and plans to partner with the institute trainees to prepare food for residents after the housing units become inhabited. The directors of all three organizations spoke enthusiastically about the institute's training program and its benefits for both employers and program participants.

Another organization that is providing pharmacy tech training gives another example of a collaborative organizational effort to provide job training and placement. Due to a shortage of pharmacy technicians, one private organization developed a six-month training program that includes three months of training that is conducted at the local center. Participants then complete three months of training on the job and a national pharmacy chain gets the first chance to hire participants as pharmacy technicians. Other organizations have responded to welfare reform changes by designing shorter training programs that will be eligible under new, shorter-term training contracts. Yet another example is a religious organization that partners with twenty-five congregations in the county to provide temporary shelter on a weekly rotation among the churches. One private organization has become a major force in developing partnerships with other nonprofits to provide job preparation and placement services. Furthermore, this organization is working with two government organizations to implement the county's new "One Stop" employment offices.

A trustee expressed concern about a lack of affordable transportation. "It's a large township. And transportation is a very—you may have a car, but it's a junker, breaking down, so they lost their job. Or they don't have, they have a suspended driver's license and no car insurance or something. They just can't afford it. Then they get further and further in debt." At least one agency is addressing this issue. The executive director reported having established a service to assist low-income families with a car purchase and insurance. Through their "Family Loan" program, which started in 1997, families can borrow up to $2,500. While the loans can be provided for other needs, the most common use has been to purchase a car.

One social service provider pointed out that private foundations usually award grants for innovative programs, no long-term, ongoing projects, but that they are now reexamining this long-standing approach to insure that funding practices achieve the funders' goals for providing the best services to meet needs.

There is a disincentive for county workers to collaborate with other organizations since they fear losing their jobs as the welfare rolls decline. In addition, welfare reform has led to the widespread use of performance-based contracts. Performance-based contracts replaced contracts in which service providers were reimbursed for delivering specific services. Contracts no longer include funding for an organization's infrastructure. However, outcomes are expensive to measure. Furthermore, evaluation can be more expensive than delivering program services. There is a need for intensive services and a case management approach to prepare those who remain on welfare to enter the competitive labor force. Agencies have added mentoring and job coaching services. "I would like to see the township trustees handle Food Stamps. There's been a couple of bills introduced in the legislature that would lean in that direction that didn't go very far. I don't think it's going to happen in the real near future. But, I think it's something that needs to be done. If I had to handle Food Stamps for my township, I would probably have to hire one additional person. Some of the townships would probably have to hire three. So, we're talking 10-12 additional people in the county to handle Food Stamps. Yet, theres tons of [Food Stamp employees] in these different locations. My people have to go either clear downtown or clear out on the eastside to pick up their Food Stamps. They could do it right here. The county expenses would go way down because you could darn near, you could almost eliminate the county Food Stamp office." The pressure to collaborate coupled with an ongoing competition among providers for funding has resulted in what one respondent labeled "coopetition" (Reingold et al. 2000). Agencies are encouraged to work together, but also compete for the most job-ready clients.

Few organizations reported having funding for treating drug and alcohol problems, which suggests that the significant contribution of substance abuse to welfare dependency has not been recognized and thus funding for substance abuse programs and services is not routinely included in contracts with welfare-to-work providers.

Assistance provided by township trustees constitutes the bulk of revenue that can be used as the local match for federal funding for welfare-to-work programs in the county. Welfare-to-Work contractors raise concerns that they are being asked to do more in less time with more difficult clients.

Many participants in the survey share a major concern about the impact of reduced government support on private and corporate funding sources. Many established organizations with various missions have augmented their programs and services to include services that are targeted toward assisting people on welfare become employed.

Welfare-to-Work might take lessons from the vocational rehabilitation model or incorporate elements from immigrant resettlement programs.

The Mixed Sites

In counties that are suburban or a mix of urban and rural communities,[4] trustees are likely to have a much closer, individual relationship with clients. The following comments from township trustees in the two counties illustrate the challenges faced by trustees in more isolated areas, the variations among trustees in different townships and trustee efforts to find assistance in the community for applicants they cannot help directly (Duggan 2000).

> Well, you know, what other social services are available here in this township, there are no others.

> Now if ya' understand where—here up north, and down south of [the capitol], and in the hills down in [southern town] and all those. Their poor relief is totally different than ours. And I know because I have friends down there. We talk about this. And, their situations are totally different. I had a trustee up here on the 18th, they wouldn't do anything!

> The strength of the trustee system is the "individuality" of it. We work in an area where we know our area. We're not thinking in just a number. Yes, I have 170, this number, and this number and this number, but is the person's number ... that person's a number because I have to put something on that piece of paper. We are close enough to 'em in a twelve mile, or ten mile area, six mile area, whatever you want to say, that we know what they're in. We know what we can do for them.

> Sometimes I've had to deny 'em, but when you deny 'em, when you deny a person, you still try to find him help. You can send it to these, like Love Chapel, They'll help ya' if you deny 'em a lot of times.

One case study county, population 64,000, is dominated by one city containing about half the county's population (Duggan 2000). The surrounding areas consist of a mixture of farmland and small towns. The county is overwhelmingly white, with only 3 percent of residents identifying as black, Asian or other in the 1990 census. Yet in recent years, the Hispanic population has grown, resulting in the creation of a new organization, Su Casa, to address the social service needs of this group. While the economy in this county is doing very well, many of the high-paying jobs associated with the auto industry are gone, resulting in lower average earnings since 1985.

Prior to welfare reform, the Local Planning Council in the county supported creation of one-stop job training and education service centers.

Since welfare reform, a "Dream Team" consisting of representatives from nonprofit social service providers, government, and business have worked with unions to design a pilot welfare-to-work training program (Duggan 2000). In addition, the "Dream Team" also created a "Wheels to Work" program in which low-income families are given donated used cars.

The county has also seen increased voluntarism (Duggan 2000). For example, the Volunteer Action Center, a United Way/City initiative was founded in 1996. Likewise, Volunteers in Medicine, created the same year, provides health care to low-income community residents. Religious-based service providers have experienced a substantial increase in demand for emergency services. Trustees also rely on these voluntary organizations. "I told you that we are going to move. We're going to have part of welfare, welfare persons, on our side. And that side also houses what we call 'Volunteers in Medicine.' It's a group of doctors, volunteers, to open up the clinic. It is just a block from the bus stop."

A community center is moving to expand its primarily social role to providing collaboration with schools and provision of adult computer education classes. Trustees are also working with the schools to provide services to low-income families. For example, one trustee reports cooperation with school officials in monitoring families.

> We know what we can do for them. I can talk to the school and say, "How are these kids doing in school? Do you see any accomplishments?" [Principal's name] has been very, very good to call and say, "they're not having enough food, they're coming to school hungry. They eat everything we feed them and more." Then we say, "here we need to go to the food pantry." And we've got some kids that need shoes, and we got some kids that need this or that. We've got some kids that need glasses. I have never bought a pair of glasses, but I have people who will do that in this township."

In another case, a trustee gives the example of a recent outbreak of lice in the schools.

> We buy shampoo by the gross. People walk in here for example and say, "My children have lice. I've been told by the doctor to get this kind of lice shampoo. I can't afford it." OK, we say, "Come on, fill out this application . . . " We decided that that does't work for a three or four or six dollar bottle of shampoo. So we got with the nurses in the program, the school district, several years ago, and said the only way for that to work is somebody explain to 'em what you have to do to make it work. And

we go ahead and buy you [the school nurses] the shampoo, you dispense it, you give 'em the education and we don't have to have the application problem. Now, all of a sudden, I think everybody and his brother has to have a bottle of shampoo. We just bought another gross and we got several hundred bottles of shampoo already this year."

Local government has changed focus to employment-related supportive services such as transportation and child care (Pennington 2000). When asked what three factors most likely explain welfare dependency and long-term poverty, an overwhelming majority of the respondents stated inadequate child care, transportation, and education. According to several respondents, the county lacks the ability to provide welfare-to-work recipients with adequate transportation services. Attempts have been made to address this concern, such as the Rural County Transit Program. However, real transportation needs have only been marginally accommodating for a very select few that live close to bus lines and work regular business hours.

One respondent that runs a day care facility has changed her operating hours to incorporate evening shifts. She reports that "we have waiting lists for certain child care, too many children and not enough space. We have done all we can to increase our service levels, including extending operating hours into the evening, but we still have waiting lists (Reingold et al. 2000)." She has increased the number of services provided on site such as parent education. Trustees have also responded to the need for child care.

Person comes in, it was like last week I think, she has three kids here. Now if I had three kids sitting here with me, I'd already had [a staff member] in here four times. If I had two kids sitting here disrupting, the interview wouldn't go very well, would it? We have a contract with the YWCA that we have, now in our second year, called Crisis Child Care. So somebody come in with three children like that on their initial intake, we say, "OK, we're gonna just take the kids, make arrangements with the wife to take care of your youngsters while we go through this process with you." The trustee would also provide this service "on a scheduled appointing or if someone has a job interview. All that has made it possible through a cooperative effort, with, between us and other agencies."

One food provider has increased the frequency with which clients are able to visit the food pantry. Other agencies have increased their referrals to other nonprofits and to the township trustees. At the same time, trustees are restricting access to food and commodities.

I don't write any food checks at all, because I have a food pantry over established in our church. The church's already established it. They have vouchers for fresh fruits and vegetables and meat. And we have two rooms full of food that our people around here supply. So I don't really write [any food vouchers.] And that has saved my township quite a bit of money."

They cannot go to the food pantry unless they are from this township. It's strictly for this township. I'm strict because I'm a quarter mile from [another county] and they think they can come in. We had 'em call from town. They'd call on Sunday and they wanted us to bring the food and then finally, I finally said, 'here this is what you're going have to do, go to [the food pantry]. They cleaned 'em out in three days. So, we had to quit that. It's strictly for this township. I tell 'em how many are in the family and if they need diapers. It is paper and feminine needs, and we have everything there. We even have two dentists in our church that provide toothbrushes, everything."

In one case study county, Easter Seals has responded to increased demands for health-related assistance by people with physical disabilities by restricting eligibility through a more detailed screening process; however, these increases in demand appear to be unrelated to welfare reform and are more likely the result of changes in the Medicaid program, local economic conditions, and changes in the composition of the elderly population (Duggan 2000). Trustees also expressed a need for health care services in the county. One trustee reported, "A serious problem that we face because in our county, we have no doctors and no dentists and no eye doctors who want to see our clients because they don't want to take, they don't wait on welfare [to pay the bill]." Another trustee has taken a personal interest in the health of low-income residents in the community. "I've taken people to the doctor, I've taken 'em to the emergency room. I've taken them to have babies. One week I had three babies due in this trailer court. I had two of my women on standby at church that would have taken them."

The Salvation Army has a weekly career counseling session with probation clients (Duggan 2000). A workforce development office trains employers in receiving the Work Opportunity Tax Credit available at the state and federal levels. Another respondent said that they are continually conversing with local business to see what skills they desire from prospective employees. This change in employment and training services since welfare reform suggests that the social service provider networks are working with private industries to develop the skills needed for desirable employment in today's economy.

According to one respondent, prior to 1996, each organization had a region that was assigned by the state and that it exclusively served (Duggan 2000). In the last three years, service provision has been transformed to an open market, with increased choices in service providers for contracting governmental agencies and for the client. In addition, government funding increasingly is contingent on collaboration and the leveraging of resources among multiple providers. In fact, many government contracts now require collaboration between for-profit and nonprofit providers. Interviews with trustees in these two counties indicated that they too are collaborating more with other social service providers.

> So people are in contact. The social service network in [small city] are in contact with each other all the time. We have a case conference, that was initiated out of this office, that first Friday of each month. Sitting at this table. Agencies come in here, and anybody's invited, they can come. For example, [one agency staff member had] a hard case, didn't know what to do with it. She calls ahead and says, "I got [client name] and his family." Well, we see if we got [client] on our rolls. If we have it, and nine times out of ten we do, we bring the file. We share that information with all the other agencies. I'll call them out of professional courtesy because we're all in the business of trying to help the family. And when they walk outta here, there's usually some kind of agreement or solution. Whose gonna be the one that's gonna bird dog this thing. You just tell us what you need (Duggan 2000)."

> We "got somebody here that is from Regional Mental Health and she has a psychiatric expertise to add to whatever we're doing. Give you an example. We had one out here in Housing Authority. Housing Authority comes to these things occasionally, too. And lice infested the facility. Preservation Partners brought the case to us. We were already familiar with it because we turned it over to child protection, and it just went, went, went. We ended up taking that—gutting for all practical—all the furniture out of that place. The Housing Authority worked with us. Took all the furniture out, got rid of it, burned it, whatever had to be done. Salvation Army provided new beds and stuff. We provided all kinds of things from this office. They all worked together (Township transcript)."

> We have an organization that's called Love Chapel, that helps with deposits. Love Chapel has taken that on as part of their ministry to the community. We've always been able to piecemeal a problem together. What I wouldn't do, there's someone else out there that will do it (Township transcript)."

> An association here in town called the Hope Ministerial Association and we keep in close contact with them on poor people that we cannot help or they overqualify or whatever. Or sometimes when, even though they may overqualify, we may help, we may pay part of it, and then we'll converse with them to pay the rest of it (Township transcript)."

> I think most things that they need are available. The thing I'm struggling with most now is to gather, and that there are agencies, the more I get into the office, there are more agencies available that I didn't even know existed. And I find out those bit by bit. I wish there was more of a central place (Township transcript)."

Through their network efforts, the County Welfare to Work Planning Council has been able to broaden awareness of the changing welfare environment. It has attempted to coordinate funding streams, and it assists nonprofit, faith-based, and secular organizations in the provision of services by providing activities such as grant assistance.

Agencies must be flexible in order to remain eligible for grants. Survey respondents have changed their eligibility requirements for services. With the more stringent eligibility criteria established by the state and federal governments, the county social service providers have had to make changes in their operation to conform to the demands of the funding governmental agencies. This general realization of internal change since welfare reform was best described by one respondent who stated, "above all we have had to become flexible (Reingold et al. 2000)." According to a number of respondents, the state has changed their goals a number of times since 1995—sometimes in the middle of a fiscal year, according to one respondent. With the continual changes, social service provider agencies have had to learn to react nimbly.

Many respondents noted the importance of joining boards. One respondent commented, "we have much better information sharing since welfare reform took place in 1995 (Reingold et al. 2000)." In addition, since welfare reform there has been an increasing trend toward volunteerism. Another important development since welfare reform is the creation of the Welfare to Work Planning Council that is lead by a County Commissioner. According to one respondent, the County Commissioners have been very involved in the past couple of years. This has prompted, as one director stated, "dialogue with the private business owners (Reingold et al. 2000)." In addition, respondents reported that they feel increasing pressure to collaborate in the hopes of accomplishing their organizational mission and goals. Many directors believe welfare reform has been successful due to the economy. Other directors point to the increased collaborative efforts of the faith-based non-profits and governmental agencies. The Welfare to Work Planning Council has implemented many collaborative plans that address the needs of the more disadvantaged population. The inclusion of the county commissioners on the board and regional efforts seem to have dramatically reduced the "turfism" we sometimes see in social service organizations.

The Rural Sites
The following introductory quotations show how well trustees know their clients in rural communities (French, and Klotz 2000), and how that knowledge, usually, results in individualized services (Township transcripts).[5]

> I know everybody by their first name, and, I know the grandad and their family. I've been here all my life. Everybody knows everybody.

> A name and an address is about all that we ask from them because we know who they are, you know.

> Most of the people are related to somebody you know, either that or they got kids in school, you know, which is confidential you can't check, but, you know, you can try and put two and two together a lot of times. Figure out who needs help and who don't.

> Well, of course you can drive by and see what circumstances are, find out what it is. When you interview, you usually have an idea of where they are living. That's one thing I try. That's my first question, "Where do you live?" Cause, I don't want to, I mean, the townships are divided. And, if they are in somebody else's township, we send them to the proper trustee. And, if they are mine, then we go from there. But if they aren't, we say, "Well, you will have to see so-and-so." And that's one of our first questions.

> It's a real close community and normally if a person has problems, the community will kick in on its own. We just had one girl that's got leukemia, with no insurance. They had a benefit dinner and auction for her to help offset her bills. That's one example of how the community will react, it's a close community.

> Every now and then you get somebody coming wanting gas for their car. Now, if it's going to get them out of town I would gladly buy it, but I don't. If I could get them out of town to stay, I would give it to them.

Both the rural counties in this study are located adjacent to suburban counties with considerable social services. For this reason, although both these case study areas are rural, residents of the county have better than expected access to quality social services in adjoining counties. Therefore, they may not be typical of other, more isolated, rural counties in the state. Rather, it is possible that residents of more isolated counties would not be as well served. The study found that in one of the counties, the organizations that were founded just before and shortly after welfare reform began in the state offer more services that are directly related to assisting persons who are making the transition from welfare to work. A major change in outlook since welfare reform has been a shift in focus from short-term piecemeal and stopgap approaches, to a longer term, holistic, and individualized approach in which clients not only join the workforce, but also become integrated into the larger community.

One of the areas of shortfall in services in both counties is the provision of affordable housing (French 2000). HUD, along with additional funding from local business and nonprofit providers, recently funded a new apartment complex. In addition, a local nonprofit recently opened a new shelter for the homeless. Finally, an expansion of an existing mobile home park will begin soon. In combination, all these projects, funded by an assortment of government, business and nonprofit money, should assist in meeting the housing needs of low-income residents of the county. In the other case study county, the County Economic Development Corporation states that access to low-income housing and social service benefits has attracted an indigent population to the county (http://www.greenet/ecodev/gcedc/htm). As a result, the county is reluctant to expand services for the poor for fear of becoming a "welfare magnet."

Employment issues are another concern (Klotz 2000). In general, it appears that few employers take advantage of state and federal tax incentives to hire welfare recipients. It is not clear whether employers are discouraged by the paperwork involved, if they feel they would not qualify for the tax credit, or if there is another reason why they choose not to participate in the program. Employers in the community complain that many job applicants lack basic skills. Also, many low-skilled workers do not stay on the job long, but often quit soon after they are hired. To address these concerns, some employers in the county offer their own training programs for new employees. Still, the skills mismatch persists. Unions, a potential source of training and apprenticeship programs, are not strong in the county and many employers, especially those in the more rural areas of the county, hire only one or two workers. One employer of low-income workers indicated that his organization notifies the county office of Workforce Development when there is a job opening. Workforce Development then searches for appropriate candidates and refers applicants to the respondent's organization. This organization has also attended some job fairs sponsored by Workforce Development.

There are a number of nursing homes and home health care providers in the county that employ unskilled or low-skilled workers, often former welfare recipients (Klotz 2000). The vast majority of nursing home employees, often 90 percent of the workforce or higher, is women. For nursing homes, increased federal Medicare coverage for home health care has reduced the need for nursing home services, which in turn has led to staffing reductions. Alternatively, it is possible that the demand for visiting health care providers, perhaps mainly to provide low-skilled homemaker services, may have increased, possibly creating job opportunities for low-skilled, primarily female workers.

Another employer of low-income workers expressed frustration that when they do hire a low-income employee, that employee often quits within a short period of time (Klotz 2000). The respondent's organization completes a number of forms and a large amount of paperwork in return for very little work on the part of the employee. Often, in the respondent's opinion, the employee lacks a valid reason for quitting the job. This organization does offer a program to train certified nursing assistants (CNAs). Applicants are paid to spend a week learning basic skills and after the successful completion of this program are hired for 75 hours of on-the-job training. After about a month on the job, the applicant prepares for the state certification test. All training services are provided free of charge and the applicant is hired after successfully completing the state certification procedure.

Likewise, skills training programs initiated in the past have struggled (Klotz 2000). For example, a home health care provider in the community sponsored a home health aide training program for several years; however, the respondent believes that the market is saturated for these skills. The program was discontinued because workers were having trouble finding jobs. A child care provider considers apprenticeships and employment training as part of the agency's mission. As a result, this provider has employed and trained a number of people who have gone on to open their own day care centers. While this approach may increase the original provider's competition in the long run, the respondent believes that there is a sufficient need for quality day care throughout the county that the competition has not yet become intense.

Trustees mentioned that employers have left the community and that it is difficult for residents to find jobs.

> I think when GE shut down up there at town in our county, that really hurt this area. And then, Sunbeam shut down up there and that hurt. I got three or four people who always worked up there, you know. We just need one good factory here (township transcript).

> They are trying to put people to work, in a lot of cases. But, here in a small town, it works great in bigger cities—where they've got more to offer people. Here, we don't have it to offer people. You know, so the re- form don't come into play here, as far as I'm concerned. In big cities, that can happen, you know, but small towns, like we are, it can't happen (township transcript).

A respondent representing a government employment program expressed concern that as a result of welfare reform and changes in national workforce development laws, the organization will service many fewer clients and receive much less funding in the future (Klotz 2000). This respondent was concerned that there will be an increasing demand for employment services. Since 1995, this organization has seen the same overall number of applicants, but a larger proportion of the clients are harder to serve and often have more severe barriers to employment.

Many employment and training agencies indicate that they only re- cently added the welfare population to their caseload (Klotz 2000). A major employment and training provider in the county began its work focusing exclusively on employment programs of disabled adults. The techniques developed to work with this population are now being em- ployed in working with the welfare population. The respondent for this agency believes that the "place and train" model that is advocated by welfare reform is much more effective than the old "train and place" model which often failed because people were trained in skills that were not needed in the marketplace. This respondent is a strong advocate of local control, believing that local welfare offices are much easier to work with than the state and federal bureaucracy. A number of providers stated that many low-income people lack basic skills and there are not enough training programs available to them. Second, many employment and training programs lack funding to help all the clients requesting services. Finally many employers do not take advantage of the tax incentives available to encourage hiring and training former welfare recipients. Another agency foresees an increased need for supported employment and training opportunities. Other agencies have hired more staff to provide vocational guidance and counseling. Many participants remarked of the need to improve such soft skills as punctuality and appropriate dress as well as improving interpersonal skills.

One organization has shifted its emphasis from job training to long-term job support services. In addition, employment and training providers are attempting to increase their collaborative efforts with the business community. Agencies have added life and job skills classes. They have worked to acquire more computer equipment, but there is an ongoing need for computer equipment to facilitate job skills training.

In this state, there are strong incentives to move everything to the local level. However, local providers may not be up to the task. One respondent believes that a positive impact of welfare reform has been that employment services are cooperating much more closely with the welfare department now than in the past. Welfare-to-work initiatives were implemented at the same time that funding for certain employment and training programs was cut, forcing greater collaboration between the two programs.

A government employment provider has increased its collaboration with nonprofit employment and training providers in the area (Klotz 2000). An example of this cooperation would be cosponsoring a job fair with the county welfare-to-work provider. Employers at the job fair were primarily from surrounding cities outside the county, requiring employees to commute or move. This respondent reported that a few people found employment as a result of the job fair. Similarly, welfare reform has resulted in cooperation between a Protestant congregation and a Catholic church. The Protestant church runs a food pantry that services families with last names in the first half of the alphabet and the Catholic church's food pantry serves people in the second half of the alphabet. Both churches provide cash vouchers to be used at the grocery store as well as frozen and canned products. In addition, the First Steps program in the county has developed a manual for social service agencies that lists all the providers in the community and where to refer people for food, housing, utility assistance, and other services.

In general, collaborative efforts appear to be effective in streamlining referrals and improving the efficiency of provision of services. Certainly at least a few of the trustees interviewed feel part of a larger network.

> Matter of fact, they're gonna have a trustee meeting, I forget what day it
> is in the next few weeks. Organization and township and community
> service s'posed to come. 'Ya know, they'll all be there (township tran-
> script).

> Oh yeah, I talked to people, especially the churches. They call me too, if
> they've got somebody's that desperate (township transcript).

Yet, another trustee feels isolated from other government providers.

> So I feel that yes, there is a gap there. There's a gap there between a
> township trustee and the welfare department. They used to, welfare and
> the trustee, worked together. And there was a welfare board and the
> trustees were on the welfare board. And it was completely different then
> (township transcript)."[6]

The government sponsored Step Ahead Council in the county has been
instrumental in reducing the duplication of services among providers by
bringing together numerous organizations to discuss and coordinate
services. In addition to the Step Ahead Council, there was also a nonprofit effort to coordinate social services in the past. One respondent representing a religious organization indicated that the church was active in
creating and supporting a community services center in 1995 and 1996.
Members of the congregation served on the board of the organization and
also volunteered to provide direct services. The intention of the organization was to coordinate services with other churches. However, the program never established itself in the community and closed after about
three years. Only the food pantry remains functioning.

Several organizations indicated that they are becoming more aware of
other resources in the community and are referring applicants elsewhere
rather than attempting to provide services themselves. For example, a
trustee commented on sharing expenses for services with a community
social service provider.

> Helping Hand is through the light company and they pay—this year they
> changed it, they pay up front ninety dollars on anybody's light bill that I
> turn in an application for. And then we match that. Last year, and all the
> years prior to this, they would pay thirty dollars, they would pay up to
> thirty dollars on a light bill and we would have to match it. Say some-
> body's light bill was forty-two dollars. They would pay twenty-one dol-
> lars, we'd pay twenty-one dollars (township transcript)."

A number of organizations have focused their mission more clearly in the face of welfare reform, often concentrating on a single service and making referrals for other services they previously provided directly. A greater awareness of other providers in the community also enhances the various social service agencies' ability to focus on a specific mission. In addition, several individuals have been key in developing their own visions for social service provision in the community, mixing creative approaches in meeting the needs of low-income families.

For the most part, half or more of the interviewed organizations collaborated with other social service providers in the community (township transcript). Twenty-one organizations have developed mutual board membership with other service providers, thirty-five have increased joint activities or programs with other service providers and forty-six have increased referrals or information sharing with other service providers. One food pantry in the county has increased its collaborations with a food pantry in the adjoining county. They are increasingly making more referrals to each other. Providers in the county are becoming more aware of other agencies in the community and as a result are making more referrals. This awareness has also allowed individual agencies to focus on a single service and has permitted agencies to expand their referral network.

Smaller, single service providers (often operated by volunteers) may often be left out of the loop as agencies respond to shifting funding sources and eligibility criteria. Among larger organizations, those that coordinated projects with for-profit organizations noted as particularly fruitful efforts to match clients to jobs. While collaboration among agencies did not necessarily eliminate unmet demand, it did seem to have a beneficial effect on staff morale. Staff members at agencies involved in extensive collaboration were more optimistic regarding progress to date as well as future potential. It may be that collaboration has a deterrent effect on burnout among social service staff.

While much collaboration is designed to improve community services and expand accessibility, some efforts at working together are designed to reduce efforts to take advantage of the system. In one rural case study county, a number of faith-based, social service organizations have instituted eligibility criteria in order to receive in-kind assistance. Specifically, one of the ministerial associations in the county created a system so that clients seeking assistance must have a voucher from the township trustee or another government agency indicating the client's need. The churches believe that these vouchers will reduce the likelihood of "double-dipping"—where families would go from church to church requesting assistance, taking advantage of charity and receiving more assistance than they deserve. This initiative began in response to increasing demand for food services following welfare reform. In the same county, since welfare reform, a church has instituted a fifty dollars per person, per visit cap on assistance in order to minimize the amount of assistance provided to individuals who are not members of the congregation.

Trustees share this concern about people taking advantage of the system.

> I'm hoping that they go forget about the trustee with welfare and just go to the welfare office. . . . there was a lot of double-dipping from people, going from one office to the other getting help. I think that has been cut down, but I think it could be cut down even more if they all just went to one place. They go to one place and get it and then they come to us and get it also. That's why you really gotta be watchful about it. But I think if they have one agency do the whole thing, you're gonna save money (township transcript).

In addition to conscious efforts to limit access, there are also limitations due to resources. While it appears that a wide variety of services are available to county residents, a number of these organizations report maintaining a wait list for services or running out of money or commodities. In addition, many of the smaller organizations interviewed provide these services in a piecemeal fashion, helping only a few families at any one time or offering assistance periodically rather than on a regular schedule. Many of the smaller agencies are run by a single volunteer. Some food pantries in the area are reducing services in response to perceived fraud ("double-dipping").

An interesting and unique response to welfare reform has been that of several home health care providers (Klotz 2000). These agencies have begun to shift emphasis from elderly care to an expanding program of in-home health care, child development, and baby wellness programs. These organizations have become increasingly involved in state programs to assist low-income mothers and prevent child abuse. For example, a respondent from a home health care provider indicates that the agency has increased the pediatric population in its caseload since welfare reform. In addition, this organization is working more closely with the First Steps program in the county. The First Steps program provides developmental services for children from birth to three years of age. In the past few years, this provider has established a pediatric home health care program that it is now marketing to a regional hospital. This response is common among home health care providers. These organizations have shifted resources away from providing elderly care and are increasingly looking toward pediatric care for revenue. At least one of these organizations also provides assistance in transitioning disabled adults into the workforce, but makes an effort not to duplicate services of other providers in the area. Unlike the home health care industry, some mental health providers are moving away from children and young adults to focus on the geriatric population. One residential care facility that had focused on drug and alcohol detoxification, now is increasingly working with elderly patients with Alzheimer's disease and other forms of dementia.

The social service delivery network in the county is stratified into three segments (Klotz 2000). The first layer is a set of several large, primarily non-profit, multiprogram agencies that serve several counties in the region. These providers are not headquartered in the county, but provide services in the county and often have one or more branch offices in the county. They often are affiliated with national or statewide organizations. These organizations are the most professional, with multimillion-dollar budgets, employing more than fifty people, many of whom have an advanced and specialized educational background, regular office hours, and full-time hours of operation. These few organizations receive federal and state contracts and grants and may also receive private grant funds. They represent the backbone of basic support services, including utility assistance, employment and training programs, and child care vouchers. People in dire need are likely to turn to these agencies first and supplement the assistance they receive from these agencies with help from organizations in the remaining two categories.

The next segment of the social service delivery network in the county is a number of local offices providing support services. These organizations tend to be located in a single office in the county, but may maintain part-time additional office space in another town in the county. They often are affiliated with a national organization or statewide program. While the first segment of the network tends to provide a number of different services, the agencies that compose this second segment specialize in providing one type of service or focusing on a particular client group. For example, these organizations may provide after-school programs for troubled youth or services to single mothers. These providers are relatively small, often with only one or two employees, but rarely with more than ten employees. At least one employee in the organization has a specialized degree or extensive practical experience working with the target population. For the most part, they maintain full-time business hours.

The third segment of the social service delivery network in the county consists of a number of agencies, often with a religious affiliation, for which social services are an auxiliary mission. This group of agencies provides the least formal services. These organizations often do not have regular business hours and are rarely open full-time. Volunteers often staff them and if paid staff is employed, social service delivery is not their main job. The staff rarely has specialized experience in working with a low-income population. In this rural county, these are the most numerous social service providers; because they operate on such a small scale, their programs primarily supplement assistance from other sources.

Conclusions and Implications

Several conclusions and implications can be drawn from the study (Reingold et al. 2000). The complexity of funding streams has hampered efficient employment and training programs. The confusion surrounding funding streams and eligibility criteria has had a concrete impact on employment and training programs. Agencies are reluctant to develop or expand employment and training programs because of the administrative rules governing funding of these programs. The federal 70/30 percent rule is particularly cumbersome. This rule sets aside the vast majority of training funds for the most disadvantaged clients. Yet, many clients with multiple barriers to employment do not fit into the narrowly prescribed eligibility criteria for 70 percent of welfare funds. As a result, these clients with considerable need must compete with other more work-ready clients for the remaining 30 percent of funds. Many organizations cited examples of welfare recipients who were turned away as ineligible despite multiple barriers to employment.

In fact, several urban county respondents indicated that they reduced employment and training services for current and former welfare recipients because their original program took longer than the government funding allowed. One well-established agency providing training in office skills lost federal contracts because the program takes more time than government funds allow. One urban county provider commented, "They [social service organizations] can't keep up with all the changing program criteria and sources of governmental funding. Service providers fall behind or don't know how to position themselves to get government funding to get people into the workforce. There are too many [funding] streams to follow (Reingold et al. 2000)." If this general confusion among providers is true, it is likely that clients are equally bewildered. This level of confusion may result in reduced levels of program participation if providers and possible clients experience difficulty in determining eligibility for various programs. In addition, the confusion may result in clients receiving inaccurate and/or inconsistent information about program eligibility and guidelines.

Related to employment challenges is the impression that the remaining welfare recipients have more problems and need more help to reach self-sufficiencyn (Reingold et al. 2000). The "work first" direction—that is the emphasis on finding a job, even a job that does not show promise of leading to full-time and well-paid long-term employment—is to some degree deplored by many respondents surveyed. These respondents fear that the time limits for receiving support while preparing for and seeking employment are too restrictive. In response to "work first," a number of agencies have either been created or adapted to get into the employment training and job search arena.

Successful agencies have been able to be flexible in the programs they offer in order to qualify for the shifting funding requirements. The administrative costs associated with tracking new (and changing) funding sources and applying for resources controlled by different government agencies, each requiring a different set of funding application criteria, has made it increasingly difficult and expensive for individual social service agencies, particularly those that do not have a close fit to the changing funding criteria, to secure resources to provide services.

Three factors were instrumental in allowing social service providers to adapt to the changes resulting from welfare reform (Reingold et al 2000). A key factor in allowing agencies to prosper in the shifting climate of welfare reform is strong links to the local social service network. Related to active participation in the local network, successful agencies are able to rapidly respond to changes in available funding. Likewise, networking promotes an agency's ability to tailor services to a new population.

A key component of successful adaptation to welfare reform is active involvement in the local social service network (Reingold et al. 2000). A formal and informal collaboration of certain social service providers constitutes this close-knit community in the county. These service providers coordinate with government agencies in order to get referrals and contracts. They may also refer clients among themselves. Several respondents felt that being a part of this network is at least partially a political process. Some respondents express concern that dissenting views are not welcome within the network. One respondent recalled voicing concern about the lack of a particular social service in the community and feeling unwelcome at subsequent meetings. That respondent's agency is no longer part of this informal local network. Other respondents whose agencies are not as involved indicate that the network is rather close-knit and clubby. As a result, these respondents believe that it is difficult to become a part of the social service network. If an agency is not part of that network, it is more difficult to survive. As a result, several respondents have mentioned that their organizations have moved away from serving the welfare population to provide programs for clients who can pay for services. Being a part of the local social service network offers opportunities for funding and expanding the agency's client base.

Successful social service agencies are able to respond to shifts in funding (Reingold et al. 2000). They can adapt to receive private funds when they previously had relied on government grants. One respondent specially mentioned that the program began with government funding, but is now able to attract private funds to continue. Steady and reliable sources of funding are key for an organization to succeed and grow. Agencies that are too dependent on a single source of funding are hardest hit by cutbacks. For example, a mental health care provider in the community is struggling to build a middle-class practice now that the public assistance office has reduced referrals. A multiservice agency has had to deny people utility assistance when a government grant was exhausted. Many respondents comment that a main reason that their agencies are not able to meet demand is a lack of funding. Successful agencies manage to maintain funding, often drawing from both public and private sources.

Finally, another successful adaptation strategy for social service agencies is to shift their mission in response to changing demands (Reingold et al. 2000). A number of social service agencies in this rural county have expanded, transformed, or refined their missions in response to welfare reform. For example, several employment and training providers who previously focused services on the disabled have added the welfare population to their caseloads. These organizations grew by expanding their caseloads. Several nursing homes and home health care providers are shifting emphasis away from elderly care in favor of child development and wellness programs. A home health care provider specifically mentioned that the need for elderly care has stabilized, but the need for home health care for children is growing. These organizations made a deliberate decision to shift to a new market. Social service agencies have also refined their missions in response to welfare reform. A number of churches in the community that previously had provided financial assistance and in-kind benefits in response to a number of different needs are now concentrating on a single service, most often a food pantry. Successful social service agencies are able to increase, modify, or focus services in response to a changing policy climate.

Appendix A: Data Collection Methods

In the spring of 1999, a mail survey was sent to all 1008 township trustees. Surveys had a numeric code that linked the respondent to his or her township. The response rate was approximately 50 percent, with 503 responses returned. After data were entered into the database, the respondents and nonrespondents were compared to determine if the two groups differed systematically in terms of poor relief spending. Statistical tests comparing the mean values of total spending on poor relief (including administrative costs) and total direct spending (less administrative costs) revealed no statistically significant difference between the two groups. Also, the ratios of all township spending (in all areas) to total spending on poor relief (with administrative costs) for all townships in the two groups were compared; again, the test revealed no statistically significant difference.

It should be noted, however, that the mean values for these variables do differ between the two groups, albeit not at the level of statistical significance. There is anecdotal evidence that a number of large, urban townships did not wish to respond to the survey. Because these townships would presumably spend more on poor relief than smaller, more rural townships, this might account for the higher mean spending among nonrespondent townships. The lower ration of all township spending to poor relief, indicating a higher percentage of township spending going to poor relief, would also be expected of larger, more urban townships. Aside from likely having higher demand for poor relief, urban townships generally do not perform functions such as property assessment, fire protection, and park maintenance, as do many rural townships.

In part, these different mean values are not statistically significant because there is extremely high variance between the townships. With values for poor-relief spending ranging from zero in many townships, to several million dollars in others, the differences in observed mean values for respondents and nonrespondents do not indicate a systematic response bias problem. It should also be noted that these data are extremely sensitive to high values in the largest townships; nonresponse by just a few of the largest spenders on poor relief probably accounts for the observed difference in means. While this occurrence is unfortunate, it is not believed to compromise the validity of the data.

In conjunction with the Community Social Service Provider component of the welfare reform study, the same six case studies in seven counties were used for interviews with both service providers and township trustees. Thirty-six interviews with township trustees in these designated counties were conducted. Interviews usually took place in the trustees' office, whether at their residence or in separate office space. About half of the trustees in each study county were interviewed. Interviews lasted approximately an hour and a half and were audiotaped with the trustees' permission. In addition, the interviewer took written notes during the interview. Twenty-nine tapes of these interviews were fully transcribed, two tapes were partially transcribed and five tapes have not been transcribed. In addition, responses to closed-ended interview questions were entered in an Excel database for analysis.

The trustee interviews are designed primarily to provide qualitative data to illustrate the findings of the quantitative data from the state administrative data and the mail survey. The interviews allowed for more in-depth exploration of the local reasons for some of the observed increases and decreases in poor relief expenditures. Being in the trustees' offices also provided a greater opportunity to observe firsthand the considerable variability in the size of the trustees' operations and the types of services they deliver.

Community Social Service Provider data are drawn from face-to-face surveys with 295 executive directors of social service agencies that provided services to current and former welfare recipients. The survey response rate was 86 percent. Data were collected from February through August of 1999 and the average length of the interview was between sixty and ninety minutes. Interviews were generally conducted at the respondent's office.

A network of field researchers collected data in the seven counties. The use of field associates is designed to make use of the local researchers' experience and expert knowledge of the communities being studied. Field associates conducted interviews in their county and were responsible for writing a case study identifying unique attributes of their community social services. The case studies include two urban, two mixed, and two rural sites. Communities were selected for in-depth investigation based on two criteria. First, researchers looked for a combination of urban, suburban, and rural communities in order to reflect potential differences based on differing geographic contexts. In addition, it was necessary to find communities easily accessible to the field researchers. As a result, all communities selected were within easy driving distance of an institution of higher learning in the state.

Ideally, field associates interviewed the executive director (or person responsible for day-to-day operations) of the organization. However, interviews were conducted even if the executive director was unavailable or assigned the interview to another staff member. The majority of interviews (207) were conducted with the target respondent. Of the remaining interviews, 19 were conducted with respondents occupying a senior executive post, 32 were conducted with less senior respondents, 12 interviews were conducted with a minister or pastor, and 25 interviews were conducted with a direct service provider.

A two-part questionnaire was used to structure the interviews. The first portion of the questionnaire consisted of primarily closed-ended questions designed to record basic descriptive characteristics of the organization, including financial information, staff patterns, and service activity. The second half of the questionnaire was open-ended, examining perceptions of welfare reform and examples of collaborative or innovative efforts.

A modified quota snowball sampling technique was used to identify participants. Initially, agencies were found through public documents such as the phone book and local listings of social service providers. In addition, respondents named social services organizations with which their organization worked and these references led to additional potential participants. Potential respondents were screened to ensure that the agency provided services to current and former welfare recipients and that the agency served the case study county. In addition, in order to ensure that the interviews included a crosssection of the social service provider community, agencies were selected based on organizational type and services provided. The organizational types include (1) public or government organizations; (2) not-for-profit, nonreligious organizations; (3) not-for-profit, religious organizations; (4) for-profit organizations; and (5) hybrid organizations. In addition, eight types of organizational activity were used on the selection of agencies. The categories were (1) counseling; (2) intermediary services for other social service providers; (3) transportation; (4) legal and civil rights; (5) housing; (6) food and health; (7) child care and youth services; and (8) workforce development and education. Because many organizations provided services across categories, field associates asked respondents to identify their primary mission and used this response to categorize the agency.

Not-for-profit organizations constituted about 72 percent of the final sample. Approximately 25 percent of the organizations are faith-based, religious organizations. Seventeen percent of the final sample are public organizations and the remaining 20 percent are for-profit organizations.

About a third (34.7 percent) of the organizations provide workforce development and training services, about a quarter (25.1 percent) provide counseling and mental health—related services, a third (33.3 percent) provide food and health services, slightly less than a third (29.2 percent) provide services for children and youth, and slightly less than a quarter (23.7%) provide housing-related services. Only about one in twenty provide legal, transportation or coordinating services (5.1 percent, 5.2 percent, and 6.2 percent, respectively).

Endnotes

[1] The chapter draws extensively from research conducted as part of a study conducted by the Indiana University Institute for Family and Social Responsibility titled "The Impacts of Welfare Reform on Community Social Services in Indiana" September 2000.
[2] Information on specific sites is taken from Karen Evans and Rebecca Van Voorhis, 2000.
[3] Quotations are taken from unpublished transcripts of interviews with township trustees, 1999.
[4] Results are drawn from field reports conducted by Lynn Duggan and Brian Pennington, 2000.
[5] Unpublished township trustee interview transcripts, 1999.
[6] Unpublished township trustee interview transcripts, 1999.

Bibliography

Byers, Katharine V., Marilyn E. Klotz, Paul Kirby, and Gaamaa Hishigsuren. 2000 September. "Final Report on Township Study of the Community Social Services Study of the Impact of Indiana's Welfare Reforms," Institute for Family and Social Responsibility. Bloomington, Ind.
County Economic Development Corporation. http://www.greenet/ecodev gcedc.htm. August 4, 1999.
Duggan, Lynn. 2000. Field report.
Evans, Karen. 2000. Field report.
French, Sandra. 2000. Field report.
"The Impacts of Welfare Reform on Community Social Services in Indiana." 2000 September. In *Indiana University Institute for Family and Social Responsibility Study.*
Klotz, Marilyn. 2000. Field report.

Nathan, Richard. 1996. "The 'Nonprofitization Movement' as a Form of Devolution." In *The Nelson A. Rockefeller Institute of Government Working Paper Series.* State University of New York, Albany.

Pennington, Brian. 2000. Field report.

Pirog, Maureen A. 2000 September. "Final Report: The Welfare Clients: Part I of the Impacts of Welfare Reform on Community Social Services in Indiana," Institute for Family and Social Responsibility. Bloomington, Ind.

Reingold, David, David Brady, and Mudit Mittal. 2000 September. "Final Report: The Social Service Provider Study: Part III of the Impacts of Welfare Reform on Community Social Services in Indiana," Institute for Family and Social Responsibility. Bloomington, Ind.

Township trustee interviews. 1999. Unpublished.

Van Voorhis, Rebecca. 2000. Field report.

Chapter 7

Douglas M. Ihrke
Richard Proctor

The Influence of Administrative Leadership and Governing Board Behavior on Local Government Innovation

Local governments have long been considered laboratories for experimenting with governmental reforms. Reforms first attempted and refined at the local level often become the standard used by other governments (Gabris, Grenell, Ihrke, and Kaatz 2000). Scholars such as Gabris and Golembiewski (1996) argue that local governments are more apt to innovate than state and federal governments because of their small size and their capacity to make decisions quickly and decisively. Political economists make essentially the same argument in their essays about the benefits of metropolitan governance. These scholars (e.g., Bickers and Williams 2001; Oakerson 1999) suggest there are particular benefits offered to citizens that are derived from metropolitan regions being governed by numerous local governments with overlapping jurisdictions.

Local governments are under increasing pressure to do more with less. Economic considerations such as tax revolts, skyrocketing employee pensions and health care costs, and diminishing aid from state and federal governments continue to challenge local governments to experiment. Yet economic pressures are not the only factors contributing to local government innovation. We feel that both administrative and political leadership play an equal role in bringing about innovation at this level of government.

Innovation may be brought about by a number of economic and political factors. However, innovation in and of itself does not guarantee success. We contend that the implementation of managerial reforms may be as important as the mere adoption of such reforms. Therefore, it is important to examine the perceptions of the success or failure of these reforms based on those who are asked to carry them out.

Innovation in local government can take on numerous forms, but some of the more recent incarnations include privatization of government services (Savas 1987), public-private partnerships (Rosenau 2000), instilling quality in government (Swiss 1992; Bosner 1992; Ingraham 1995), reinventing government (Osborne and Gaebler 1992), and reengineering processes (Hammer and Champy 1993; Ihrke 2000; Ihrke, Rabidoux, and Gabris 2000). Other innovations in local government include treating the citizen as a customer (Denhardt 2000), implementing formal strategic planning technologies (Bryson 1995), and instilling a profit-oriented focus (Savas 1987). Many of these innovations may or may not be considered those that are developed by policy boards, but rather by administrators working for policy boards.

The "who" in who develops policy may not be as important as the "how" in how those policies are implemented. Research by Ihrke and Lombardo (1999) suggests that the most important factor in determining how successful city councils are in representing constituent interests is the evaluation of how well those very councils do in delivering programs and services. These researchers argue that at least at the local level, the evaluation of governmental effectiveness has as much to do with how well policies are implemented as it does with the specifics of those policies and who worked to develop them.

While we know that local governments are likely to engage in innovation, we do not necessarily know what contributes to the perceived success or failure of those innovations. The central focus of this chapter is to explore the factors that contribute to managerial innovation in local government. In particular, this study attempts to examine how administrative leadership and local governing board behavior serve as intervening variables affecting the perceived success of these reforms.

In this chapter we explore the evaluative perceptions of local government department heads with regard to success or failure of governmental reforms. The data for this study come from a survey of local government department heads working for Wisconsin municipalities (N = 57) with populations greater than 10,000.

Literature and Hypotheses

The challenges faced by local governments in the deficit centered years during the 1970s and 1980s are well documented. Local governments were faced with increasing budget shortfalls due to factors such as decreasing intergovernmental revenues from the federal and state governments. It was also during these years that central cities faced major shortfalls in property tax revenues due to the flight of middle-class residents moving to suburban communities. Those who were left in central cities were the least able to pay for municipal services and municipalities were forced to act, mainly by cutting programs and services to citizens.

The 1970s and 1980s were also years in which American industry faced increasing competition from foreign manufacturers. The American auto and electronics industries were particularly vulnerable during this time. During this same period, observers of governments also became critical of governmental waste. Stories of exorbitantly priced toilets and hammers filled the newspapers.

Scholarly works critical of inefficiencies in government were also published during the late 1980s and early 1990s. One of the more popular works was Peters and Waterman's (1982) *In Search of Excellence*, where the authors highlighted companies that have transformed themselves through various innovations to meet customer needs and preferences. Local governments in the 1980s also began experimenting with the privatization of a number of city services as a means for reducing costs and instilling competition (Savas 1987). An emphasis on quality also characterized this era, as illustrated by the popularity of Total Quality Management, a management paradigm first developed by Edwards Demming (1986). Osborne and Gaebler's (1992) reinventing government initiatives also caught on when President Bill Clinton signed on to the National Performance Review (NPR) under the leadership of Vice President Al Gore. Hammer and Champy (1993) received a good deal of attention as well with the publication of their book, *Reengineering the Corporation*. These authors challenged public and private organizations to examine their process systems used to develop products and services as a means of cutting down on inefficiencies.

The popularity of these and other works published during this era has led to a renewed interest among scholars and practitioners on economy and efficiency in governmental service provision. On the surface, the level of innovation emanating from governmental organization seems to be at its highest in a number of decades. The question becomes: What explains the relative success or failure of these reforms?

We argue that positive perceptions of managerial innovations are largely a function of the perceived credibility of administrative leaders (Gabris, Grenell, Ihrke, and Kaatz 2000), as well as the level of conflict on city councils, an argument first articulated in the works of James Svara (1990, 1995) We further argue that perceptions of innovative success are a function of the effectiveness of the relationship between city council members and administrative staff. Generally, we argue the more local administrators are perceived as credible leaders (Gabris and Ihrke 1996; Kouzes and Posner 1988, 1995), the better governing board members are able to manage board conflict (Svara 1990), and the more positive the nature of the relationship between board and staff, the more likely managerial innovations will be perceived as successful by key local government actors. We specifically explore a number of hypothesized relationships between managerial innovation and leader credibility, board member relations, and board-staff relations that will be outlined next.

James Kouzes and Barry Posner (1988) have identified five broad practices and ten basic commitments of leaders who have been identified by their followers as exhibiting credibility. These practices and commitments are listed in Figure 1.

Essentially, these authors argue that when leaders practice these behaviors and carry out these commitments, their followers tend to believe they are credible. Credibility, in turn, leads to what the authors describe as the ability on the part of leaders to get extraordinary things done in organizations.

Figure 1 Kouzes' and Posner's Practices and Commitments of Credible Leadership

Challenging the Process
1. Search for opportunities
2. Experiment and take risks

Inspiring a Shared Vision
1. Envision the future
2. Enlist others

Enabling Others to Act
1. Foster collaboration and trust
2. Strengthen others

Modeling the Way
1. Set the example
2. Plan small wins

Encourage the Heart
1. Recognize individual contribution
2. Celebrate accomplishments

Research studies indicate that leadership credibility makes a difference in terms of both individual and organizational outcomes. For example, Gabris and Ihrke (1996) and Ihrke (1996) have found a significant relationship between the credibility of leaders and subordinate burnout. In a small study of Illinois local governments, Gabris, Grenell, Ihrke, and Kaatz (2000) found a significant relationship between leadership credibility of CAOS (i.e., mayors or city managers) and city council conflict. Their study indicates that as department head perceptions of CAO credibility increase, perceptions of city council conflict decrease. We therefore hypothesize that department heads that perceive their administrators to be high in leadership credibility will perceive managerial innovations to be more successful than those department heads who perceive their administrators to be low in leadership credibility.

A number of studies have explored the effects of city council conflict on the behavior of city managers, most of which have been based upon the seminal work of James Svara who argues that city conflict on city councils leads to poor decision making for local governments. For example, James Kaatz, P. Edward French, and Hazel Prentiss-Cooper (1999) find in their research a significant relationship between city council conflict, job burnout, and city manager turnover. James Kaatz (1996) also found a stronger relationship between assertive managerial behavior and turnover than between city council conflict and turnover. Ruth Dehoog and Gordon Whitaker (1990) found in their study of Florida cities that city managers who left their positions "experienced considerable frustration with council conflict" (p. 161). Dennis Barber (1988) found that approximately 9 percent of the city managers in his study left their positions to escape a negative work environment. Using data from the 1991 Municipal Form of Government Survey, published by the International City/County Management Association, Tari Renner and Victor DeSantis (1994) found that mayoral and city council member stability in office lead to increased job stability for city managers.

In this study we argue that city council conflict is significantly related to department head perceptions of managerial innovation. Too much conflict on councils can be time consuming for managers to deal with, which can ultimately affect their ability to innovate administratively. Highly burned-out managers are unlikely to innovate, and department heads will likely pick up on the feelings and perceptions of their managers and respond accordingly. Conflict on city councils is likely to limit the perceived effectiveness of managerial innovations. Based on the research that has been done on city council conflict, we hypothesize that as conflict increases, department head perceptions of the success of managerial innovation decreases.

Legislative officials have become increasingly reliant on the expertise of administrators, a trend that has been well documented in the twentieth century (e.g., Mosher 1982; Stillman 1996). City councils serve as legislative bodies for local governments. Department heads, whether under the direction of mayors or city managers, are asked to interact regularly with council members. The oversight responsibilities of city councils require them to receive regular updates from department heads as to what they are doing within their respective domains. Interaction between department heads and council members is thus by design.

City councils have been known to intervene into the affairs of department heads, particularly since department heads are directly responsible for providing local government services. Council members represent constituents through various means, including what political scientists have coined as "casework." Casework involves responding to complaints and inquiries from citizens who are concerned about issues such as water bills, missed garbage collection, and police protection. Oftentimes council members will directly contact department heads to inquire about these and other situations. At times, these contacts can be divisive as department heads may feel council members are intervening in their affairs.

The oversight and casework responsibilities of city councils can lead to strained relationships between council members and department heads. When city council inquiries into the performance of department heads becomes invasive, relations can deteriorate between these local government officials. When this situation arises, it is also likely that relations between the council and the CEO have diminished since department heads are directly responsible to CEOs. It is highly unlikely that the department head will perceive the CEO as effective since they may feel they are unable to do their jobs due to city council interference. Therefore, we hypothesize that as city council relations with department heads decrease, so will department head perceptions of the effectiveness of managerial innovation.

We test these assertions, as well as a number of others relating to managerial innovation using data from a survey of department heads working for municipalities in Wisconsin.

Data and Method
The data for this study were collected in the summer of 1998 via a survey mailed to department heads working in Wisconsin municipalities (N = 57) with populations greater than 10,000.[1] A total of 561 surveys were mailed to department heads, of which 183 were completed and returned for a response rate of 32.6 percent. However, at least one department head from 55 of the 57 cities responded to the survey, thus making for a revised response rate of 96.5 percent. The survey consisted of a series of statements relating to various local government administrative innovations, CAO leadership skills, and policy board (city council) attributes. The respondents expressed their relative agreement with each individual statement using a five point Likert scale, with a 1 representing "strong intense disagreement" and a 5 representing "strong, intense agreement."

We examine the department heads' evaluations of leadership credibility, internal policy board conflict, and board-administration relations on the effectiveness of various managerial innovations. We hypothesize that perceptions of greater leadership credibility and more cooperative relations between the board and the administrative staff will be viewed as leading to more successful managerial innovations, in the opinion of the department heads. We also propose that greater levels of board conflict will limit the perceived effectiveness of administrative innovations The specific innovations that we examine are efforts to employ a profit-oriented focus, efforts to treat the citizen as a customer, and efforts to employ formal strategic planning techniques. Stated formally, the specific hypotheses we examine are as follows:

> H1. The perceived success of managerial innovations is **positively** related to the perceived credibility/effectiveness of the city manager/mayor.

> H2. The perceived success of managerial innovations is **negatively** related to the level of conflict on the policy board.

> H3. The perceived success of managerial innovations is **positively** related to the effectiveness of the relationship between the policy board and the administration.

To devise the variables to be examined in the above hypotheses, indices were created by grouping department head responses to several statements that related to a particular measure of interest for this study, for example, leadership credibility. The responses to the grouped statements were then averaged to create that particular index.

Indices were created for attributes that are perceived to influence the success of managerial innovations: leadership credibility, policy board conflict, and board-administration relations. Indices were also developed to proxy for two of the specific innovations examined in this study: treating the citizen as a customer, and employing formal strategic planning techniques. A single variable was used to measure efforts to instill a profit-oriented focus in local government.

To illustrate, leadership credibility was measured using an index developed by Gabris and Mitchell (1991). The index is an equally weighted average of the department head's responses to eight statements relating to leadership skills and attributes, including, for example, "the CEO clearly communicates the purpose and rationale behind new programs and reforms in a way that wins employee acceptance and board approval," and "the CEO follows through on promises regarding changes and reforms he/she expects others to carry out." The alpha reliability coefficient for the leadership credibility index was .91, thus indicating a high degree of internal consistency. The other indices were created in a similar fashion, with each index developed from the responses to three to six related statements.[1,2] The alpha reliability coefficients for these indices ranged from a low of .66 for the "citizen as customer" index, to a high of .89 for the "formal planning" index.

To test our hypotheses, multivariate regression analysis was employed. We first looked at department head assessments of managerial innovation in general, and we then considered their evaluations of specific managerial reforms such as treating the citizen as a customer. We regressed each of the managerial innovations on the factors that we believed would influence the perceived success or failure of the innovations, and examined the significance (and sign) of the coefficients.[1]

Results and Discussion

Before managerial reforms can be successful, administrators must first take actions to implement them. Therefore, we first looked at whether leadership credibility, board conflict, and board-administration relations are believed to influence CAO attempts to implement managerial reforms. We utilized these measures in a regression model, using as the dependent variable department head responses to the statement "This organization continually strives to practice the most recent state-of-the-art management technologies." The results are presented in table 1, under "attempted innovations." They indicate that of our three hypothesized determinants, the only significant factor is the leadership credibility (LCI) of the CAO.

Table 1 Multiple Regression Analysis of the Local Government Attempts to Implement Managerial Reforms and Their Success

Dependent Variable:	Parameter Estimates[a]	
	"Attempted Innovations"[b]	"Innovations Successful"[c]
Independent Variable:		
Intercept	1.359*	.941
Leadership Credibility Index	.396***	.447***
Policy Board Conflict	-.100	.0141
Board-Administration Relations	.135	.152
Adjusted R^2	.163	.193
F-statistic	12.765***	15.322***
N	182	181

[a.]   * $p < .025$, ** $p < .01$, *** $p < .001$; for one-tailed test of hypotheses.
[b.]   Dependent variable statement: "This organization continually strives to practice the most recent state of the art management technologies.".
[c.]   Dependent variable statement: "On balance, the [managerial] reforms attempted by this organization can be described as 'highly successful.'"

There is clear support for the argument that an effective leader at least attempts to employ the latest managerial reforms. However, there is no evidence that department heads believe that the policy board's internal or external relationships either help or hinder CAO attempts to implement managerial innovations.

It is not enough that a CAO merely attempt to implement managerial reforms; for an administration to successfully serve the public the innovations must be implemented successfully. We next looked at the perceived influence of leadership credibility, board conflict, and board-administration relations on the perceived success of managerial reforms in general. We used a regression model with the dependent variable measuring department head responses to the statement "On balance, the [managerial] reforms attempted by this organization can be described as 'highly successful.'" The hypothesized predictors were again the indices measuring leadership credibility, board conflict, and board-administration relations. The results are presented in table 1, under "reforms successful." The results indicate that of the three factors hypothesized to influence the success of reforms, again only leadership credibility is significant. These results suggest that the dominant influence on the adoption and successful implementation of managerial reforms is the credibility and effectiveness of the CAO as a leader. City council member relations among themselves or with the administrative staff do not appear to affect the adoption or effective implementation of managerial reforms in general.

We next examined the influence of leadership and board relations on specific types of managerial innovation. While our previous results indicated that policy board relationships did not significantly influence the success of managerial reforms in general, it is conceivable that its temperament, in both internal and staff relations, may affect the success or failure of specific types of innovations. We therefore examine the relationships between department head evaluations of CAO leadership credibility, board conflict, board-administration relations, and the perceived success of several specific managerial innovations. The innovations that we considered here are efforts to employ a profit-oriented approach to providing services, efforts to treat the citizen as a customer, and efforts to employ formal strategic planning techniques. We regressed each of these managerial innovation indices on our three hypothesized influence measures. The results are presented in Table 2. To test our first stated hypothesis (H1), that the perceived success of managerial innovations are positively related to the perceived credibility of the administrative leader's effectiveness, we examined the coefficients on the LCI in each of the 3 models. The coefficients are positive and significant, in accordance with our first hypothesis, and with our original findings. There is consistent evidence that higher perceived leadership qualities are associated with higher levels of perceived success for all three types of managerial innovations examined. Department heads who believe that their CAOs are more credible and effective leaders also believe that their innovations are in turn more successful.

Table 2 Multiple Regression Analysis of the Perceived Influence of Leadership Credibility, Board Conflict, and Board/Administration Relations on Specific Managerial Innovations

	Parameter Estimates[a]		
Dependent Variable:	Profit-oriented[b]	Customer Service-oriented[c]	Strategic Planning-oriented[d]
Independent Variable:			
Intercept	1.816**	1.794***	1.911***
LCI	.230**	.342***	.34***
Policy Board Conflict	-.0439	-.102	- 182*
Board-Admin. Relations	.223*	.171**	.190*
Adjusted R^2	.102	.301	.271
F-statistic	7.846**	26.989***	23.090***
N	18	182	179

[a] * p < .025, ** p < .01, *** p < .001; for one-tailed test of hypotheses
[b] Complete dependent variable statement: "This organization has succeeded in developing new programs and services that have generated self-supporting revenues."
[c] Customer Service Index
[d] Strategic Planning Index

To test our second hypothesis (H2), we looked at the coefficients on the policy board conflict index in the same regression equations. The only significant coefficient was in the model looking at the perceived success of formal planning techniques, thus only partially supporting our second hypothesis. Contrary to our conjecture, conflict among the board members does not influence the perceived success of efforts to privatize services, or efforts to treat the citizen as a customer. One explanation for this may be that the implementation of formal strategic planning methodologies requires the ongoing, active participation of the policy board, in the same way that strategic planning in the private sector is a primary function of a corporation's board of directors. Internal disagreement among board members over the appropriate strategic path to follow may prevent the successful development and implementation of a coherent, consistent, and therefore successful, strategic plan. On the other hand, the successful development and implementation of profit-oriented and customer service efforts do not require much "hands-on" participation by the policy board; the specific programs will be developed by the CAO and administrative staff. Therefore, the board's internal squabbles may have less impact on these managerial innovations.

To test our third hypothesis (H3), we examine coefficients on the policy board-administration relationship index in table 2. All of the coefficients are positive and significant, supporting our contention that the better the relationships are between the board and the administrative staff, the more successful the managerial innovations are perceived to be.

From these results we can conclude that, according to the department heads, the mere adoption of managerial innovations in local government is not sufficient to ensure their success. Effective leadership in implementing the reforms substantially increases the likelihood that the innovations will be considered successful. In other words, CAOs need to do more than just "talk the talk," or adopt whichever managerial innovation is currently in fashion, and assume that its successful implementation is a foregone conclusion. They must also "walk the walk," or provide effective, credible leadership to ensure that the reform is considered to be successful. Additionally, the department heads believe, based on their experiences, that a well-functioning relationship between the policy board and the administrative staff further contributes to the successful implementation of managerial innovations. However, for those innovations that do not require active, ongoing participation by the policy board, it does not appear that the department heads view board conflict to be a significant deterrent to the successful implementation of managerial innovation.

Conclusions
In this study we attempted to better understand the factors that aid or hinder managerial innovation in local government. Our findings indicate that the credibility of the CAO goes a long way in both adopting and

successfully implementing general managerial reforms. Credible leadership helps to guide local governments toward innovation as well as in ensuring its success. These general findings provide support for those who have raised concerns about the lack of leadership in local government and what it might mean in the future as local governments are being asked to do more with less.

Leader credibility was also found to be important in determining the success or failure of specific managerial reforms, in this case implementing a profit-oriented focus in government, strategic planning, and efforts to treat the citizen as a customer. While credibility involves envisioning the future or inspiring others, two characteristics of Kouzes and Posner's leadership model, it also seems to involve following through with the implementation of new ideas and reforms, at least in terms of the perceptions of department heads directly accountable to CAOs in Wisconsin.

Conflict on city councils has received a great deal of attention in both newspapers and scholarly works. Divisiveness on city councils seems to be on the rise as more and more interests are attempting to get their voices heard through their local representatives. As the country becomes more diverse, conflict may increase even more as minority groups will attempt to get their fair share of public goods. We thought conflict would filter down into the administrative ranks of local government organizations in a way that would hinder managerial innovation. We were only partially correct in this assertion as we found city council conflict to be unrelated to the adoption and implementation of general administrative reforms in government, and only negatively related to one specific reform—strategic planning. Thus it seems city council members tend to keep their personal differences to themselves and these differences do not seem to affect managerial innovation.

Our findings reveal no significant relationship between board-administrative relations and the adoption and implementation of general managerial reforms. Our study indicates that general innovation may very well remain within the domain of CAOs, and influenced little by the relations between city council members and administrators. In other words, general innovation starts with the leadership of the CAO, and may very well end there as well. However, our findings indicate that board-administrative relations make a significant difference in terms of specific managerial innovations.

Board-staff relations make a significant difference in terms of focusing on the bottom line (profit-oriented), emphasizing the needs of the customer, and strategically planning for the future. Congenial relations between board and staff seem to lead to more successful innovations in administration. These innovations have largely been borrowed from the private sector, and administrators may very well be influenced by council members who have used them in the organizations for which they work in their regular jobs.

Our hope is that these findings will be of encouragement to those concerned about helping local governments rise to the standard of excellence. Leadership and board behavior do make a difference in terms of local government innovation. But our story is incomplete in that we have in no way uncovered all there is to know about innovation in local government. Future research should, for example, explore the relationship between local government finance and managerial innovation, as economic conditions will undoubtedly influence managerial behavior. Furthermore, other scholars may want to consider relationships between managerial innovation and factors such as government structure and interest group influence, to name a few.

Appendix
Statements Comprising the Indices

Treating the Citizen as a Customer:
1. This organization has a clear and known emphasis on treating the citizen as customer.
2. The organization uses modern technologies for acquiring customer input such as customer surveys, focus groups, town meetings, or similar "formal" and systematic mechanisms.
3. Employees and board members of this organization have received special training in customer service.
4. This organization has attempted to implement a formal total quality management (TQM) program to enhance service quality.
   $\alpha = .66$

Formal Planning Index:
1. This organization has utilized more advanced strategic planning technology to frame its mission and priorities.
2. This organization has conducted stakeholder analysis and a thorough environmental analysis of its strengths, weaknesses, opportunities, and threats [SWAT analysis].
3. This organization has a clear, updated mission statement.
4. This organization engages in and utilizes regular goal-setting sessions for the policy board.
5. This organization prioritizes goals annually and plugs these goals into the budgetary process.
6. This organization has a strategic plan that includes both short-term and long-term issues.

$\alpha = .89$

Leadership Credibility Index (LCI):
1. The CAO (chief administrative officer) clearly communicates the purpose and rationale behind new programs and reforms in a way that wins employee acceptance and board approval. The CAO actively works to communicate the organization's vision and mission to employees, and works hard to ensure they understand the rationale behind the vision and mission.
2. Developing a shared vision and set of core values is a fundamental objective of the CAO.
3. Employees feel they can trust this CAO and feel comfortable putting their fate into the hands of this administrator.
4. When assigning projects and responsibilities, the CAO makes sure employees have sufficient power and authority to accomplish the assigned objectives.
5. The CAO practices what he/she preaches in terms of values, work effort, and reforms. He/she sets a good example for others to follow.
6. The CAO follows through on promises regarding changes and reforms he/she expects others to carry out.
7. The CAO actively seeks to reward, praise, and recognize high performance. The CAO lets employees know when they are doing well.

$\alpha = .91$

Policy Board Conflict
1. Conflict among some board members is high.
2. Sometimes, disagreements between board members get in the way of making decisions.
3 Disagreements between board members or between board members and the CAO often become personalized.
4. Some disagreements between board members seem to go on for ever.

$\alpha = .86$

Policy Board/Administration Relations
1..Communication between the policy board and administrative units/administrators is frequent and effective.
2. When the board makes decisions, administrators faithfully carry out the policy according to Board intentions.
3. On balance, the Board views its relationship with administrators as a team, rather than as a supervisor telling someone what to do.
4. Staff feels comfortable interacting with the Board, especially when giving it information that may be controversial or that it does not want to hear.

$\alpha = .79$

Bibliography

Barber, Dennis M. 1988. "Newly Promoted City Managers." *Public Administration Review* 48: 694-699.

Bickers, K. N., and J. T. Williams. 2001. *Public Policy Analysis: A Political Economy Approach.* Boston, Mass.: Houghton Mifflin.

Bosner, Charles F. 1992. "Total Quality Education." *Public Administration Review* 52 (5): 504-512.

Bryson, John M. 1995. *Strategic Planning for Public and Nonprofit Organizations.* San Francisco, Calif.: Jossey-Bass.

DeHoog, Ruth Hoogland, and Gordon P. Whitaker. 1990. "Political Conflict or Professional Advancement: Alternative Explanations of City Manager Turnover." *Journal of Urban Affairs* 12 (4): 361-377.

Deming, Edwards. 1986. *Out of Crisis.* Cambridge, Mass.: MIT Press.

Denhardt, Robert B. 2000. *The Pursuit of Significance.* Prospect Heights, Ill.: Waveland Press.

Gabris, Gerald T., and Robert T. Golembiewski. 1996. "The Practical Application of Organization Development to Local Governments." In *Hand
book of Local Government Administration,* ed. Jack Gargan, pp. 71-
101.

Gabris, Gerald T., and Douglas M. Ihrke. 1996. "Burnout in a Large Federal
Agency: Phase Model Implications for How Employees Perceive Leadership Credibility." *Public Administration Quarterly* 20: 220-249.

Gabris, Gerald T., and Kenneth Mitchell. 1991. "The Everyday Organization: A
Diagnostic Model for Assessing Adaptation Cycles." *Public Administration Quarterly* (Winter): 498-518.

Gabris, Gerald T., Keenan Grenell, Douglas M.Ihrke, and James Kaatz. 2000.
"Managerial Innovation at the Local Level: Some Effects of Administrative Leadership and Governing Board Behavior." *Public Productivity and Management Review* 23 (4): 486-494.

Hammer, M., and J. Champy. 1993. *Reengineering the Corporation.* New York,
N.Y.: Harper Business.

Ingraham, Patricia 1995. "Quality Management in Public Organization." In
Governance in a Changing Environmen, ed. Guy Peters and Donald
Savoie. Montreal: McGill-Queen's University Press.

Ihrke, Douglas M. 1996. *Burnout in a Large Federal Agency.* Ph.D. dissertation.
Northern Illinois University. Ann Arbor, Mich.: Dissertation Abstracts.

Ihrke, Douglas M. 2000. "Local Government Innovation: Some Effects of Administrative Leadership and City Council Behavior." Poster presented
at the American Political Science Association National Conference.
Washington, D.C.

Ihrke, Douglas M., and Salvatore Lombardo. 1999. "Representational Effective
ness in New York State Local Governments." Paper presented at the
Midwest Political Science Association National Conference. Chicago,
Ill.

Ihrke, Douglas M., Greg Rabidoux, and Gerald T. Gabris. 2000. "Managerial
Innovation in Local Government: Some Effects of Administrative
Leadership and Policy Board Behavior." Poster presented at the Mid-
west Political Science Association National Conference. Chicago, Ill.

Kaatz, James B. 1996. *City Manager Tenure Stability: A Predictive ModelBased
on Perceived City Council Conflict, Leadership Effectiveness, and
Conflict Resolution.* Ph.D. dissertation. Northern Illinois University.

Kaatz, James B., P. Edward French, and Hazel Prentiss-Cooper. 1999. "City
Council Conflict as a Cause of Psychological Burnout and Voluntary
Turnover among City Managers." *State and Local Government Review*
31 (3): 162-172.

Kouzes, James, and Barry Posner. 1988. *The Leadership Challenge.* San Francisco, Calif.: Jossey-Bass.

Kouzes, James, and Barry Posner. 1995. *Credibility.* San Francisco, Calif.:
Jossey-Bass.

Mosher, Frederick. 1982. *Democracy and the Public Service*, 2nd edition. New York: N.Y.: Oxford University Press.

Oakerson, R. J. 1999. *Governing Local Public Economies: Creating the Civic Metropolis.* Oakland, Calif.: ICS Press.

Osborne, David, and Ted Gaebler. 1992. *Reinventing Government: How the Entrepreneurial Spirit Is Transforming the Public Sector.* New York: William Patrick.

Peters, T., and R. Waterman. 1982. *In Search of Excellence*. New York, N.Y.: Harper.

Renner, Tari, and Victor DeSantis. 1994. "City Manager Turnover: The Impact of Formal Authority and Electoral Change." *State and Local Government Review* 26 (2): 104-111.

Rosenau, Pauline Vaillancourt. 2000. *Public-Private Policy Partnerships*. Cambridge, Mass: MIT Press.

Savas, E. E. 1987. *Privatization: The Key to Better Government*. Chatham, N.J.: Chatham House.

Stillman, Richard. 1996. *The American Bureaucracy: The Core of Modern Government.* Chicago, Ill.: Nelson-Hall Publishers.

Svara, James. 1990. *Official Leadership in the City*. New York, N.Y.: Oxford University Press.

Svara, James. 1995. *Facilitative Leadership in Local Government*. San Francisco, Calif.: Jossey-Bass.

Swiss, James E. 1992. "Adapting Total Quality Management." *Public Administration Review* 52 (4): 356-362.

Endnotes

[1] The city of Milwaukee was excluded from this study due to the size and complexity of its political structure.

[2] See Appendix for a complete listing of the specific statements used to create each index.

[3] An index was originally created for the profit-oriented measure, based on the responses to 3 statements; however the alpha reliability coefficient was only .43. Therefore, we substituted the responses to one of the specific statements in place of the index. The regression results obtained from using this one statement are qualitatively identical to the results obtained from using the index, and the quantitative results are practically identical.

[4] Given our hypotheses, all of the tests are one-tailed.

Chapter 8

Conclusion

Michael Harris
Rhonda Kinney

In the introduction to this volume we argued that given the wide array of societal and political changes impacting American governments through out the late twentieth and early twenty-first centuries, we might fruitfully reexamine the policy innovation process and its correlates at the state and local level. This reassessment seemed particularly timely given the burgeoning interest in innovation and change-centered leadership in the corporate arena. Given the increasing overlap between these areas of theory and practice, we hoped to draw together policy studies and these new areas of insight and development.

We argued that a careful reexamination of the topic might help us to better understand the motivators and inhibitors of the innovation process as well as more thoroughly connect policy innovation to insights found in the broader public policy research literature. To help in this task, we offered a flexible framework (displayed below in figure 1) designed to summarize an array of hypothesized relationships. The framework demonstrates the multiplicity of ways in which variables impact and weave their way throughout the innovation process. It brings a dynamic and interactive perspective to the innovation process that we believe more accurately reflects the innovation process at the state and local level.

As suggested in the introduction, we return in this concluding chapter to this overarching framework in order to access the degree to which the model we proposed proves helpful in contextualizing and more fully understanding the contributions made by the volume's case studies and analyses. We focus our attention on what we consider to be areas of particular interest: the central importance of economic conditions in motivating and driving the demand for policy innovation, the role policy entrepreneurs play in converting these opportunities into concerted action towards particular solutions, the role of institutional design and cross-institutional relationships, particularly the vital interplay, and diffusion across levels of government. We touch briefly on the role other variables play at different stages of the policy process. This includes the relationship of such items as political party control, ideology, and public opinion to the policy innovation process. Finally, throughout these discussions, we attempt to integrate insights drawn from the broader public policy literature—specifically, the policy stages heuristic—into our understanding of policy innovation.

Figure 1 Model of Policy Innovation Process

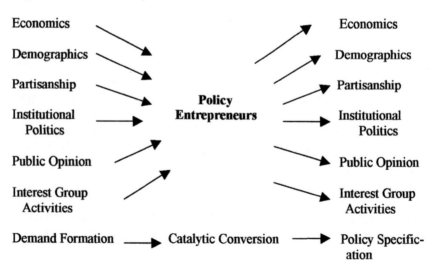

Economic Conditions

Motivating Factors
In the introductory chapter of the volume, we argued that economic factors were necessary factors in motivating innovative change. We also suggested a disagreement was present in the literature between those who felt innovation was spurred by slack, unused resources and those who argued that economic problems and scarce resources were the type of "problems" that motivate significant policy change. The case studies and analyses presented by the chapter authors provide a good deal of insight on these issues for the time period addressed here.

Clearly, economic variables constitute important factors in the innovation processes assessed in the preceding chapters. Several of the chapter authors presented evidence of the role these factors play in motivating and sustaining change. Some also noted the ways in which a lack of economic resources affected the demand and conduct of change.

In his chapter examining education policy, Michael McLendon offers evidence that supports a relationship between a governmental unit's limited resources and the drive to implement innovate policies. He suggests that in the area of education governance, "conditions of economic scarcity . . . serve as a powerful catalyst for policy innovation by state governments" (52). He further argues "the prospect of further economic decline in both states, coupled with already stagnant economies, helped 'trigger' interest among policy elite for innovation in higher education governance . . . Second, innovation in higher education governance became politically feasible when other policy options for stimulating the state economy (tax reform, additional budget cuts, or the consolidation of state agencies, for example) themselves proved impracticable" (52). So in the area of education policy, states were motivated by current limited resource levels as well as by a desire to encourage future economic growth. This suggests that governments respond to retrospective and prospective evaluations of economic conditions. This expands the dialogue regarding whether creative policy innovation is driven by the presence of slack economic resources or by conditions of economic scarcity. We argue that McLendon's analysis suggest a need to more carefully specify the efforts of government to address current economic conditions delineating them from attempts to prospectively impact future developments.

Like McLendon, Richard Chard's chapter highlights the need for detailed specification of economic pressures on government. His findings suggest significant impacts for both general conditioning issues such as holding down of government budget size as well as for more specific problems and challenges. Chard's analysis of Medicaid across U.S. states also offers further evidence that limited resources will spur innovation. His analysis focuses on tight state budget dollars as potential motivating factors in the policy innovation process. His study "supports the notion that states develop innovative policies when motivated by budgetary pressure to control costs. Interestingly, however, his study shows that even in the absence of specific economic pressures, "states will adopt policies enacted in neighboring states that have reduced costs (76)." While we will comment further on issues of diffusion in the below section specifically on this topic, it is worth noting now that as suspected, economic factors serve as necessary, but often not sufficient conditions for significant policy change.

Chard's chapter also adds a further dimension to our understanding of the factors relating to policy innovation. While other chapters focused on the overall state or local economic environment, Chard hones in on program specific economic factors such as cost per program enrollee and number of individuals enrolled in the program. This point closely connects with our introductory comments on the need to articulate more clearly characteristics of the programs and policies under analysis and the need to specify relationships between these characteristics and other related variables.

We found the relationship between economic factors and policy innovation to be robust across the other cases presented here as well. Each of the cases found evidence linking either scarce resources or a need to grow or revitalize economically to the decision to innovate. Lawrence Grossback suggested that "the economy and fiscal stress played a key role in the adoption of new mandate policies in Minnesota and in the effectiveness of their innovations." Specifically, economic pressures at the local level push these governments to demand change from the state. "The economy also appears to have influenced the implementation of Minnesota's key mandate innovation, the waiver program of the Board of Government Innovation and Cooperation."

Robert Stoker discussed Baltimore's efforts to develop institutional mechanisms to support the city's classification as an Enterprise Community. The Empowerment Zone/Enterprise Community initiative "designated the Department of Housing and Urban Development (HUD) as the lead federal agency for the urban sites and emphasized the importance of mobilizing local communities to develop solutions to the problems of economic renewal and community revitalization." And finally, Ihrke and Proctor cite the degree to which local governments are under increasing economic pressures—tax revolts, skyrocketing employee pension and health care costs, diminishing aid from state and federal governments. Only Klotz did not specifically posit a relationship between economic conditions and the policy changes she studied. She does, however, note that economic conditions in the state were improving at the time welfare reforms were actually implemented and that demands placed on the program declined throughout the time period she studies in the chapter.

Clearly the large preponderance of evidence indicates that at least during the decade of the 1990s economic scarcity and the drive to spur slacking economic growth correlate with state and local policy innovation. However, the evidence also clearly demonstrates that as expected, while economic factors are vital and necessary to change, they are not sufficient in and of themselves to spur policy change. They provide the impetus but may not provide enough motivation on their own to affect change. This reality is somewhat different than in the private sector. Since government does not go out of business as a result of inefficiency, the pressure of economic realities is less than in the private sector. To what degree this thesis is a catalyst for innovation and change remains an open question. A better understanding of the degree to which economic factors drive innovation and change in the public sector is a challenge for further investigation.

Stages and Design of the Policy Process

Not only are economic factors important in motivating and driving the demand for policy innovation, many of the cases presented in this volume suggest that the particulars of the economic situation are related to the policy alternatives that are considered, the process for implementation, and its current phase. As we suggested in the introduction, the development of policy alternatives is an important question that has not been given much attention. How many alternatives were considered, why these alternatives were considered and not others, and what was the process of choosing the selected alternative? Furthermore, it is important to understand what variables and constraints were considered while developing the plan for action. The chapters offered in this volume fruitfully illustrate this point.

For example, Michael McLendon connects the economic nature of the demand for change to the specific need to *decentralize* school governance in Hawaii and Illinois. McLendon's analysis suggests decentralization may be viewed not simply as a governing philosophy but also as an attempt by these states to shift costs and ongoing demands to another level of government. This trend is quite similar to the nature of many changes at the federal level throughout the 1980s and 1990s—efforts to decentralize control and responsibility for programs correlate with efforts to shift program costs and decrease the size of the federal budget deficit.

Grossback also mentions that the presence (or absence) of economic resources will impact effective implementation. He notes "the Board of Government Innovation and Cooperation was forced, in part, by a lack of resources to focus on grant making for policy innovations rather than on taking the lead in studying mandates in order to make recommendations for their removal from state law" (95).

Bob Stoker notes that Baltimore created a nonprofit, quasi-public corporation, Empower Baltimore, to manage their empowerment zone/redevelopment initiative and act as liaison between the empowerment zone and the city and state governments. The corporation's mission—"to foster sustained economic opportunities within the Empowerment Zone and to build communities in ways that give Empowerment Zone residents greater access to and readiness for those opportunities." Their efforts moved forward on two fronts—business related programs (attract new businesses) and resident services (develop the workforce). Stoker adds that "the greatest limitation that constrained this initiative was community capacity. The problem is that distressed communities tend to lack civic infrastructure, the institutions and leading citizens that stabilize and organize the community to make things happen" (110).

We have safely concluded that economics matter in the initial stages of the innovation process. However, we have now identified the fact that economic conditions also affect the selection of a specific policy. The challenge we face is to identify other factors that impact the selection of an innovative policy. We believe that identifying these variables and an analysis of the policy selection will have a significant impact on our understanding of innovation in the public sector.

Policy Entrepreneurs

The framework we presented in the introduction and repeated hypothesized that policy entrepreneurs oftentimes play central roles in catalyzing the demand for change into a drive to innovate in a more specific fashion. Much of the recent literature in the policy studies area focuses on this central role and the business literature we cited has centered on the importance of leadership in the innovation and change process. We did, in fact, find in the case studies presented here a good deal of support for the importance of entrepreneurs in the policy innovation process. This finding is of interest as it is consistent with our knowledge of the private sector. It may suggest that not enough attention is given in the literature on public sector innovation as to the role of the entrepreneur.

In his study of Minnesota's innovative governing boards, Grossback cited the central impact of a mandate task force organized by a local government leadership association as well the role of the Citizen's League in the creation of one of the state's governing boards. McLendon also argued that policy entrepreneurs play important catalytic roles in the education policy innovations he analyzes here. Namely "a university president in Hawaii and a governor and lieutenant governor in Illinois were especially influential in the processes of issue redefinition and interest mobilization" (54). Ihrke and Proctor noted that "economic pressures are not the only factors contributing to local government innovation. We feel that both administrative and political leadership play an equal role in bringing about innovation at this level of government." They go on to argue that long-term relationships among city council groups and city leaders impact the ability of leaders to successfully innovate. Their analysis suggests that board conflict is related to lower leadership credibility and this lowered standing results in less successful innovation over time.

While entrepreneurs are not explicitly discussed by Stoker in his presentation, his case inspires questions about the ways in which leadership and/or entrepreneurship can be motivated, created, and sustained when a large number of players are involved in a policy effort. This case offers a number of overlapping and multidimensional relationships that create difficulties over time. Entrepreneurship contributes to the development of specific policies, but at times many players are involved, with many visions and many limits that may not always effectively integrate.

Clearly, significant evidence exists indicating that entrepreneurs and effective leadership matter in this process. However, unlike economic conditions, these factors may not be a necessary condition for innovation to occur. However, they are a key factor in driving innovation. The degree to which entrepreneurs impact the process of innovation is an important question and one that we cannot answer at this point. However, we believe the role of entrepreneurs in the development of innovated policy is underestimated. Further, as we suggested in our introductory chapter, studies of change-based leadership in the literature on private-sector innovation and leadership will likely provide important and relevant insight into these questions.

Institutional Relationships

Diffusion and Endogenous Factors

As we discussed in the introductory chapter of the volume, one of the central questions in the policy innovation literature to date has been the degree to which diffusion of innovative ideas occurs across unit borders. Corollary questions include the pattern such diffusion might take and whether or not some geographic areas or governmental units are more or less innovative than others over time. We hoped to examine related questions in the cases examined here; we did in fact observe a number of cases where diffusion was present. However, here again, cross-state pollination was not enough in and of itself to drive the desire and attention to innovate. Further, diffusion tended to affect other stages of the policy-making process as much as, and sometimes more than, the initial demand formation stage.

Richard Chard's chapter on Medicaid policy innovation provides an interesting picture of interstate policy diffusion in that he suggests some forms of innovation—specifically, cost containment strategies like managed care—may diffuse irregardless of other political and economic factors at work. The drive to contain certain costs appears almost independent of other political and economic forces pressing on governmental actors in this area.

Grossback finds evidence supportive of a cross state diffusion process along with the importance of internal variables. He suggests that Minnesota policy makers find ideas and guidance from other states in the specification process (not at the demand stage). McLendon also finds that although other studies have documented that higher education policies do migrate across state borders, in the two case studies he presents here dealing with governance innovation, endogenous economic and political forces were the "primary drivers of policy innovation" (53).

Diffusion is also found in the local level studies we presented. Stoker questions the factors related to the specific form of innovation in Baltimore. He cites as examples of this phenomenon history and experience with similar institutional structures applied to other circumstances. In our previous work in the area of Medicaid reform in Michigan we argued a similar point. There, pilot projects in one small area ten years earlier gave the state guidance for how they might address the larger reform effort they hoped to undertake later on. In Baltimore, previous experience with nonprofit, quasi-public corporations fed development efforts in community redevelopment.

These issues lead us to conclude that in the future we might profitably examine diffusion in more broadly defined ways. Clearly, cases exist (some included in this volume) where diffusion occurs in the expected manner across geographic and governmental units. However, as some of the other case studies offered here illustrate, other potential modes of diffusion may exist as well. For instance, we might look to see if diffusion occurs *across* policy arenas as well as across units *within* a particular policy area. This is especially relevant if we choose to consider processes as well as particular policy specifications as "innovative." Cost containment strategies might then diffuse from health care to crime management or from education to community development—the list goes on and on. Our analysis here certainly suggests that this possibility is worth additional examination. We also believe that it is of importance to pay attention to the role leaders and entrepreneurs play in this process. To what degree do the relationships and informal relationships impact this process.

Intergovernmental Incentives

Our introductory comments questioned the impact of intergovernmental incentives on the innovation process. The chapters presented here offer a degree of support for the importance of these relationships and incentive structures in driving the innovation process. The specific issues dealt with by chapter authors ranged from the impact specific financial incentives from one governmental level to another, to intergovernmental mandates, to issues of communication, coordination, and implementation.

Richard Chard focused on the central importance of the relationship between federal and state governments in the efforts at innovation in Medicaid policy. The willingness (or lack thereof) of federal officials to grant waivers allowing innovations in approach or design set the boundaries of what states could accomplish. While other factors likely drive demand for innovative change at the state level, the ability to act on that demand and the specific limits in devising and selecting policy alternatives are sometimes strongly related to intergovernmental factors.

Lawrence Grossback's careful review of state-local mandates in Minnesota also offered substantial insight in this area. His chapter examined mandates and their impact as well as the state's attempt to construct innovative responses to the objections to original policy mandates. Demand for change at the state level was driven to a large degree by local government opinion and lobbying efforts on behalf of reform. Klotz's chapter dealing with the implementation and impact of welfare reform further demonstrates the ways in which local government and nonprofit agencies respond to incentives provided by the federal government. Agencies were "reluctant to develop or expand employment and training programs because of the administrative rules governing funding to these programs" (153), Along with Chard's chapter, these case studies suggest that while each level of government continues to a level of independent discretion, incentives offered intergovernmentally influence the policy process in important ways.

Grossback's analysis further suggests that as a result of complex intergovernmental relationships the process of problem definition can oftentimes be far more complex than traditional models of innovation and reinvention suggest. His cases highlight that different levels of government may disagree at times over whether or not a problem actually exists, or what the dimensions, nature, or root of a problem may be. This creates unclear demands for action and makes policy making difficult.

Stoker's chapter on Baltimore's efforts to institutionalize policies related to the creation of citywide Enterprise Zones points out the role federal funding and related policy prescriptions have on impacting city and state efforts to implement policy change. Clearly the creation of the federal program in 1993 provided an initial impetus in this case. However, the legislation's lack of specificity about how best to mobilize or continue momentum throughout the ten-year-long period from development to final implementation of the programs hindered the success of the program over time.

We can clearly see the impact of intergovernmental incentives as well as the consequences of demand driven by one level of government (federal) while implementation occurs at another (local). Future policy makers must be mindful to create clearer relationships in this area and to establish procedures for implementation in order to effectively achieve objectives. The literature on intergovernmental relations and federalism could prove to be valuable in developing a better understanding of intergovernmental incentives.

Other Political and Demographic Variables

In the introductory chapter, the model we presented posited effects for additional contextual variables including multiple political and demographic factors. These factors were not universally addressed by chapter authors but some variables of note did come up in their analyses. Interestingly, some of the references were to null findings in unexpected places.

McLendon, for example, suggests that his study of higher education governance in Hawaii and Illinois provides little evidence of a differential party effect in this policy area. The Democratic regime in Hawaii and the Republican regime in Illinois appeared equally willing to experiment with decentralization in this arena. Similarly, Chard argued that political party control at the state level is not significantly related to the degree to which states seek and receive Medicaid waivers. He went on to say that differences in state education levels also do not relate to variation in this area. While we do not have enough evidence yet, these studies suggest that political and contextual factors are relatively less important in the innovation process than one might first think.

Grossback cites the level of commitment displayed by officials as contributing significantly to the success of efforts to implement innovative policy changes. Because many state leaders were not committed to the goals of innovative programs, implementation of programs has been slow to occur.

At the local level, Klotz points to the importance of organizational flexibility to the change process. Organizations displaying flexibility and a willingness to revisit mission and procedures were more likely to adapt well to the specific changes characterizing welfare reform. Further, Klotz notes the importance of community social networks in aiding new program implementation. Her chapter suggests that successful adaptation to welfare reform is related to active participation in these networks.

Given that political and other contextual factors have been recognized as important variables in understanding policy making in the public sector, we are unwilling to argue that they matter less than economic conditions or leadership activities. The cases presented here reinforce that variables beyond economics and leadership affect innovative activities and policymaking. The analyses suggest that developing and understanding innovation requires attention to local political realities. Future research must flesh out these issues in additional detail.

Consequences of Broader Definition of Innovation
Given the attention we paid to this issue in our introduction, we want to offer brief comments about the consequences of our use of a broader notion of policy innovation in this volume. Our definition allowed us here to examine issues that might have been left out of more traditional studies and some of the more exciting areas of policy making throughout the 1990s. The chapters presented here analyze process changes in current policy programs and institutions—not simply additions of new policy programs. This expansion allows inclusions such as Chard's chapter on Medicaid reform that analyzes a program whose constituents and providers remain constant but whose provision process is substantially revised.

The broader definition also allows us to focus on issues of governance in higher education rather than simply outcomes. Our decision to include process and implementation changes also provides an opportunity to examine intergovernmental mandates and enterprise zones as well. We believe others may have included these innovative approaches as well. However, we suggest that our careful attention to conceptualization of the term "innovation" symbolizes a larger commitment in our study to broader notions of the policy process than that provided by previous research studies in the area.

Summarizing Items for Further Study
The studies presented here, along with previous research on innovation suggest a relationship between economic conditions and the long-term success of the implementation process for innovative policy change. We can reasonably conclude that economics, particularly conditions of economic scarcity, influence all phases of the policy-making process. Economic factors play a significant, and likely necessary role, in spurring innovation. However, the cases analyzed here also leave us with clear needs for more research. For instance, once the economic impetus for change fades, will the demand for the innovative policy remain in place? For some policies, the answer is clearly yes. Many newly created innovative federal programs of the 1960s and 1970s, such as Medicaid and the Head Start program, become quite entrenched entities over time. Other innovative changes appear to lose steam when economic conditions change. A case in point may be state-level efforts to comprehensively integrate managed care into health care programs such as Medicaid and Medicare throughout the 1980s and 1990s. Implementation efforts seem to ebb and flow as economic conditions go up and down over time. Future research on policy innovation might further investigate and specify the nature of these relationships in the implementation stage of this process.

As mentioned above, more research needs to be done on the endogenous political and contextual variables that affect innovation. McLendon's study highlighted the issue of political competition, suggesting that embattled gubernatorial regimes may be more likely to consider policy innovations than regimes under less pressure. He suggests that this "finding also lends support to the notion that politicians experiment with new policies at times within their election cycle that are most politically advantageous (Berry and Berry 1999; Mintrom 1997; Mooney and Lee 1995). We have already cited a need to more specifically discuss and evaluate the impact of political party variables, public opinion, and demographic variables. Many more likely exist and may depend on policy arena or geographic area. These questions deserve further attention in future research.

As we noted above, Grossback suggests a more careful look at the process of problem definition. He observed disagreements between levels of government in their views of the nature and degree of perceived problems. This relates closely to our assertion that we must flesh out models of innovation such that they include more stages of the policy process. Future research might focus on topics such as how the agreement or disagreement in this process may spur or hold back innovation. We might also look at how governments might structure such definitional processes in order to facilitate or slow change. Grossback also notes that research tends to conceptualize problems as unidimensional when typically they are more complex. He further cites the need to connect this with an understanding of how the characteristics of issues relate to the process of innovation and reinvention?

Stoker's analysis highlighted the importance of effective implementation. The federal Empowerment/Enterprise Zone effort and the city's own efforts were successful innovations in that unique programs were created and additional services provided. However, the programs witnessed a real lack of effective coordination between and across governmental and community groups involved in the efforts. How might we better coordinate across governmental levels and between governmental/nonprofit and corporate and other community levels? His discussion reinforces our argument that more needs to be done to incorporate an understanding of innovation into all phases of the policy-making processes. As we cited in the introduction, we argue that policy termination might also be conceptualized fruitfully as one form of innovative activity and models of innovation brought to bear on its study.

Stoker's comments also connect to questions of leadership and cooperation we have raised throughout the volume. Studies of innovation might explore questions similar to those raised by scholars studying the private sector. We are especially interested in how governmental leaders at all levels might proactively encourage and shape innovative activities.

Finally, given our interest issues of trust and confidence in government and their relationship to innovative policy activity, we find interesting questions arising from Ihrke and Proctor's chapter dealing with the issue of how one can analyze the "success" of innovative programs. They suggest that "innovation in and of itself does not guarantee success. We contend that the implementation of managerial reforms may be as important as the mere adoption of such reforms. Therefore, it is important to examine the perceptions of the success or failure of these reforms based on those who are asked to carry them out." In fact, they explicitly link the success of innovations as largely a function of perceived credibility of administrative leaders. For us, this suggests that the audience—citizens, clients, and constituents—for innovation may be as valuable in this analysis as the actors that carry our innovation.

As the political, social, economic, and technological environment continues to change in a rapid fashion, more attention must be given to the role of innovation in addressing those challenges. The purpose of this study was to focus scholarly attention and expand understanding on issues of innovation in the public sector. We hoped to pay particular attention to economic issues as well as to individual and group leadership activities. Private sector interest in innovation, entrepreneurship, and change leadership continue to expand over time, and this study was intended to bring that focus and attention to the analysis of governmental policymaking. This volume successfully addressed several issues but we also brought to light a number of interesting questions that future research can build on. We have demonstrated that the framework we provide here will be useful in organizing additional questions and findings as well as better understanding and contextualizing findings from future studies in this regard.

Bibliography

Berry, Frances Stokes, and William D. Berry. 1999. "Framework Comparin Policies Across a Large Number of Political Systems." In *Theories of the Policy Process,* ed. Paul A. Sabatier. Westvie3 Press: Boulder, Colorado 169-200.

Mintrom, M. 1997. Policy Entrepreneurs and the Diffusion of Innovation. *American Journal of Political Science* 42: 738-770.

Mooney, C. J., and M. H. Lee. 1995. "Pre-Roe Abortion Regulartion Reform in the U.S. States: Diffusion, Reinvention, and Determination." *American Journal of Political Science* 39: 599-627.

Index

Wright, David, 106-107

Yin, R. K., 39-40

Zaltman, Gerald, 12, 17
Zimmerman, Joseph F., 83-85
Zumeta, W., 33

About the Editors

Michael Harris is Associate Provost and Professor of Political Science, specializing in Public Policy and Public Administration, at Eastern Michigan University (EMU). Harris was awarded the Michigan Association of Governing Boards Distinguished Faculty Award and has been recognized for excellence in teaching by the American Political Science Association and by EMU. He has published two books, *Public Policy and Electoral Reform: The Case of Israel* (2000) and *Term Limits* (2001), with Gideon Doron. Harris has been published in a variety of journals and has contributed chapters to several edited volumes. In addition, he acts as a political commentator to a variety of broadcast and print media in the United States and Israel. Harris received his Ph.D. in public policy from Indiana University, his master's degree from Tel-Aviv University, and his undergraduate degree in economics and business administration from Bar-Ilan University. He resides in Ann Arbor with his wife and three sons.

Rhonda S. Kinney is an Associate Professor and department head in the political science department at Eastern Michigan University. She teaches courses in American political institutions, leadership, and policy-making processes and has been recognized for excellence in teaching by the American Political Science Association following a similar recognition by EMU's Alumni Association. Her research interests center on institutional leadership, change processes, and agenda setting, particularly in American national politics. Kinney's research has appeared in a variety of journals and in several edited volumes on public policy making. She received her Ph.D. in political science from the University of Iowa in 1996. She currently resides with her family in Ann Arbor, Michigan.

About the Contributors

Academic Affiliations

Michael K. McLendon, Vanderbilt University

Richard E. Chard, University of Hawaii at Manoa

Lawrence J. Grossbeck, West Virginia University

Robert Stoker, George Washington University

Marilyn Klotz, Center for Governmental Research,
Rochester, New York

Douglas M. Ihrke, University of Wisconsin-Milwaukee

Richard Proctor, Sienna College